MAKE THE LEAP

MAKE THE LEAP

Success, Failure, and Other
Hard-Won Lessons of Leadership

INGAR SKAUG

with

JON GANGDAL

Center for
Creative
Leadership®

CENTER FOR CREATIVE LEADERSHIP
Greensboro, North Carolina
www.ccl.org

Published by CCL Press
Sylvester Taylor, Director of Assessments, Tools, and Publications
Peter Scisco, Manager, Publication Development
Stephen Rush, Editor
Shaun Martin, Associate Editor
Kelly Lombardino, Rights and Permissions

Cover design by Redding Communications, Inc.

CCL Number 002449
ISBN 978-1-60491-184-8

CONTENTS

PREFACE:
A VOYAGE OF DISCOVERY

On December 31, 2010, I stepped down as Group CEO of Wilhelm Wilhelmsen ASA (today, Wilhelm Wilhelmsen Holding ASA). As I walked out the main door of the shipping company offices in Lysaker for the last time as an employee of the company, I felt both relief and sadness—the same feeling as when your children leave home. No matter how much both you and your children planned and hoped for that day, it is the end of something that will be gone forever.

Perhaps it is only the loss of the feeling of interdependence that connects you closely to one another but at times frays your nerves. It's not that you lack sympathy or love; it's more the feeling of powerlessness that happens to all close relationships when you weigh the responsibility that forever rests on the other party. You can seldom do anything about it—at best, you can only influence it.

I had led a corporation that, at its peak, had 28,000 employees worldwide. Now, I would only manage myself. Perhaps my conflicted feeling was due to a dawning suspicion that suddenly I was not indispensable. Even though I never worked to preserve my positions, but took management responsibilities and assignments most advantageous to me, I still had power that—as with many other intoxicating substances—can become addictive. The trick, therefore, is to quit in time.

Eventually I began to enjoy the feeling of freedom even though I quickly discovered that my life as a pensioner did not mean the easy life—quite the contrary. With a dozen board positions—some of which were very demanding—along with other duties, there was more than enough to do. But it was a good feeling; I felt that the love of work was still there.

Like most people approaching the age of discretion, I began to reflect on how I actually spent my life, especially my long life as a leader. These reflections were probably also prompted by one of the most exciting positions I held—chairman of the board of the Center for Creative Leadership (CCL), a U.S.–based, global provider of leadership development. I was one of its clients in the early 1980s, something that has always been to my benefit.

Unlike many other global companies and institutions and their branches, CCL is an ideal organization where all profits go to development, research, and charitable work. Their vision is simple: "To advance the understanding, practice and development of leadership for the benefit of society worldwide." It could be translated as: To promote the understanding, practice, and development of leadership for the benefit of organizations all over the world.

Now I can contribute even more actively to this vision, which is completely in line with the most important things I've learned after over 43 years in the business world: great leaders create great corporate cultures that help everyone on the team thrive and perform better.

As a young manager, I often chased results. I rarely took time to meditate on the three most important questions a manager should ask: "Why did this result turn out the way it did?" "What did we do well?" and "What could we have done differently and to our advantage?"

Of course, I sensed the answers, but not clearly enough that they gave me a lasting and valuable lesson. Only after things turned out very badly would we ask, "What shouldn't we have done?" or "What should we have done differently?"

Eventually I learned that a manager's main task is not to give the best answers but to establish a corporate culture of asking good questions—both in good times and bad. By changing business values and work methods into a continuous learning process, I discovered that it was possible to make decisions more quickly because we didn't need to have all the answers on the table before we began a project. As long as we initially asked the right questions—and had the feeling that we were on the right path—most often the rest of the answers we needed in order to succeed fell into place along the way. These answers would never have occurred to us if we had not already started.

Inevitably, we made mistakes. And, like everyone else, I dreaded it when I was forced to acknowledge that we had messed up. It didn't take me long to realize that if a manager wants to achieve results, he must dare to fail. Managers and employees alike must be allowed to make mistakes, as long as they don't keep repeating the same mistake. And, more importantly, as long as there is transparency about the mistakes—all the way up to the top management level. Those experiences can then be used to develop basic values and best practices so that mistakes that could lead to discrepancies can be spotted in advance.

No one makes only right or wrong decisions, just as no one is only good or evil. The trick is to make more good decisions than bad ones and to be able to adjust for less successful decisions along the way and afterward. It's that simple—and that difficult when you don't have the answers in advance!

In retrospect, it is easy to mostly dwell on the results, whether they reached great heights or ended in fiasco. But what was it that really happened? Is it possible to find some common denominators in the decisions, processes, and actions that led up to the highest peaks? What distinguished what we did—or didn't do—when we were on ground level? And are there any similar patterns behind those that ended in fiasco?

This is what I will try to determine in this book: to go on an organizational voyage of discovery through the two big companies where I had various and progressively central management positions for over 30 years—SAS Airlines and the Wilhelm Wilhelmsen Maritime Group. In each of these examples, both companies developed in completely different directions. While Wilhelmsen is still progressing and delivering solid results, SAS is on the edge of collapse after many years of adversity.

Along the way, I expect to discover something regarding how I developed as a leader—for better or worse. What expectations did I have, an only child sent around the world at a young age on my own, to become the rallying point a leader needs to be? When was my leadership a beneficial tool to put into place all the processes that customers, suppliers, shareholders, employees, and the entire team needed to perform efficiently? How did I act when I got the best out of my colleagues? What caused me to become impatient when I tried to maintain progress and got out of step with the team? And how did I manage to get back in step?

As I wrote the introduction to this book, I, of course, had some ideas of how I did it. But I still don't have the answers; I rarely had them when I approved decisions that I knew would be catastrophic if things went wrong. Even then, I intuitively knew the right thing to do. I'm quite sure that it wasn't just dumb luck that my decisions were most often the correct ones. Rather the opposite. When I overrode intuition with reason, things often went south, whether it had to do with hiring, contracts, or projects. Why? Most likely because I reasoned my way to an answer before I actually knew the solution.

Recently I came across a book by the great German poet Rainer Maria Rilke, *Letters to a Young Poet*. It contains an experienced poet's advice to a doubting, aspiring poet and is really a beautiful little piece of leadership. In one place he writes, "Don't search for the answers which could not be given to you now because you would not be able to live them. The point: to live to the fullest. Live the questions now. Perhaps then, someday far in the future, you will gradually, without even noticing it, live your way to the answer."[1]

I think that can stand as a motto for this book, which probably would not have existed had it not been for my coauthor, Jon Gangdal; Angelika, my wife and best advisor throughout our many years; and many good friends who have helped with advice and assistance along the way.

Høvik, August 2016

---

[1] Translated by Arild Batzer. Dreyers Kulturbibliotek, 1969.

1

FROM FIRE TO ASHES

I felt as though I were back in the season in those few moments when I had time to register that the leaves on the trees around our house had turned yellow and fallen from the trees. It was October 1989. The cool autumn air—always a herald to the joys of winter—came in raw and cold from Holtekilen and reminded me that another summer was over.

It eventually dawned on me that I was tired and worn out—perhaps also content. After almost 15 years of constant restructuring at Scandinavian Airlines (SAS), I had wrestled the old airline company into what became one of the world's best and most profitable airlines. Such success had obviously taken its toll.

As CEO of SAS Norway, I was satisfied with the results we had achieved. But the job was still a rat race. I was almost never home, sat in meetings in Stockholm with the executive committee every week, and held meetings with my own people all over Norway the rest of the week. The dream of a quiet family life at Høvik, only a short distance from my office at Fornebu, had disintegrated long ago. The situation was almost worse than those years when I lived someplace else. At least then I was gone when I was gone and home when I was home. Now, I was gone even when I was home. So close—and yet so far.

According to the new strategy, SAS was to become "One of Five in 95"—that is, one of the world's five largest and most profitable airlines by 1995. The search for new markets, smarter solutions, and cutting costs would be further intensified. We knew there was still a considerable market open in Denmark, Norway, and Sweden, but the huge opportunities for business growth existed beyond the borders of Scandinavia.

The new level of ambition meant, first and foremost, additional endless organizational rounds for me. SAS Norway alone had 12 unions that had to be involved in the slightest change that might affect the employees. In essence—all changes. In addition, we struggled with middle managers who still hadn't hopped on board the new way of thinking within the airline companies. That was the cost for having leapfrogged over them during the first major round of customer orientation of SAS in the early 1980s. This middle management layer amounted to what we still somewhat contemptuously called the *Rockwool-layer* of the organization, where a number of managers clung to their increasingly porous positions.

More than once, I've thought about how much energy there is in people's resistance, especially resistance that has been allowed to fester for many years. If we had only taken up the fight against this resistance from the start! Get everyone on board *with* the team—and those who wouldn't join in, *out* of the company. It was a huge mistake to let them sit on the sidelines. They just sat there and waited like spectators at a sports event. Every time someone made a mistake—which of course happened—they ganged up on the poor performer who had tried to take independent responsibility instead of following the old guidelines where decisions were pushed upwards in the hierarchy. There's a kind of power or force with people like that, a counterforce.

More and more often, I thought, "What more can I accomplish in my position?" SAS, Braathens, and Widerøe shared the Norwegian airline market: a good combination. It was just the right competition for the Norwegian inland market; only small margins would be gained by capturing a larger market share in Norway. Besides, we would have to deal with both local and national authorities, who, with regard to the special Norwegian market, maintained the principle for cross-subsidies between good and bad routes. To add to the mix, we had increasing competition from foreign airlines.

After leading the SAS turnaround in the United States from 1984 to 1986 and nearly four years at SAS Norway, I was hearing hints that my next SAS job had a Stockholm address. I had also served on the five-man group that, in practice, had driven the restructuring process together with the CEO. Several people told me that they could see me in the position as CEO of the entire company. But Janne Carlzon's position was safe. He was an important motivator in executing the company's ambitious new strategy, and had a well-functioning and capable management team around him. At the age of 46, I was, perhaps, the one in the group that had the longest future in front of me, but it wasn't a given that I was the most obvious candidate to take over.

Had my career been my only concern, it would have been an appealing job. Just being an SAS employee at that time was an honor, regardless of the position. The thought of managing a business boasting the highest reputation in all of Scandinavia, and that was targeted to capture even more parts of the world, could have easily enticed me and made me forget both travel days and organizational re-plays—if I'd had such ambitions. But I did not.

I had no doubts that SAS would succeed in achieving its new targets, although it would be a tough fight both internally and externally. SAS was not alone in wanting to compete in the international market. All major airlines wanted a piece of the new, deregulated, air-travel pie that had grown big and fat during the economic upswing of the 1980s. Ever since I signed my first corporate contract as a ticket-selling SAS trainee in Chicago in 1977, I had learned that the joy of reaching a goal is directly proportional to how much you struggled to reach it. And although I occasionally felt tired, I was absolutely *fit for a fight.*

But I couldn't see myself in the role of chief executive of SAS, perhaps because it seemed more like a position than a job. Therefore, although hints kept coming my way, I didn't consider it as a possibility. Nor did I consider that a continued career at SAS would require that I again move to Stockholm after my family and I had finally settled down in Norway where we preferred to stay.

How many times had I uprooted the family because of my SAS jobs? Our three sons were born in three different countries. They had spent their childhood as little cosmopolitans. No sooner had they settled down and found new friends than we were off to a new country where they had to repeat the same process.

I probably hadn't even noticed much of that since I had been on the road most of the time no matter where our family was based. The children weren't so distant that they didn't enjoy being with their dad when he was home. But my good and wise wife helped me understand that this wasn't okay.

So when I got a call from a headhunter at the ISCO Group hunting for a new manager to fill a challenging position in Norway, it wasn't difficult to ask to be invited to a preliminary conversation. At the least, I wanted to hear what the job was about.

Wilhelmsen Lines (WL) needed a new chief executive officer. The shipping liner company was in the trough of a large wave after two rounds of debt negotiations. But no sooner had the company been rescued before it became the victim of a new tragedy.

On September 8, 1989, more than 50 WL employees were en route from Oslo to Hamburg in a Convair 580 plane they chartered from Partnair, a charter airline company. They had been chosen to go to a ship's naming ceremony and were looking forward to some festive hours in the German maritime city. Just north of Hirtshals, the pilot lost control and crashed into the sea. All 55 on board lost their lives. Over half of the casualties included the shipping company's management. Inadequate maintenance and a broken "pirate" metal bolt holding the tail rudder caused the accident.

Knowing I was needed and would be building a business from scratch, so to speak, along with family considerations, weighed heavily on my decision. And yet, I had some doubts. I was coming from a very successful SAS and could continue to fly upward toward new heights. WL had gotten some shots across the bow but seemed to be through the worst of the rough seas. But with my aviation background, what guarantees did I have that I would be able to develop a shipping company?

In confidence, I discussed the possibility with several good friends. Because they were split right down the middle, they were of no help. Half thought I was crazy to leave SAS to be the skipper of "a tiny freighter." The family situation would most likely work out, as it always had.

The other half felt I was ready to take on a new job, not the least of which would include having more time for the family. Yes, the job was much smaller. But in return, there were greater possibilities. Besides, WL was an international company. With my experience, I could have my cake and eat it too.

It took over two months for me to make up my mind. Based on rational thought, the choice was impossible. No matter what arguments I came up with for or against the two jobs, I couldn't make up my mind. The pros and cons for both jobs were equal—just as my friends had reasoned.

During all the rational deliberations, I felt more and more drawn to WL. It was neither a positive nor negative feeling, but I knew intuitively it was the right decision. Over the years at SAS, I had learned to listen to and trust my intuition—not only when in doubt, but also when making many important decisions.

Back then, I hadn't the faintest idea that SAS was, in fact, already close to reaching its zenith and would soon enter 20 years of turbulence, almost crash landing by the time I started this book.

Nor did I know that during the same period, WL would become one of the world's largest roll-on/roll-off (Ro-Ro) shipping companies with speed along all the routes SAS dreamed of flying as "One of Five in 95." And not only there, but on all the world's oceans.

I signed the contract with WL on New Year's Eve at the office of the ISCO Group on Oscars Street. Until then, I hadn't dared show up at the shipping company office at the end of Roald Amundsen's Street for fear of starting speculation while I was still CEO of SAS Norway.

After the contract was signed, I went down to the office to look at my new workplace. It was a complete downer. I had come from the SAS building at Fornebu, with its glass and steel and large bright surfaces, where the furniture was modern, white and gray, and the vast majority of employees had computer screens at their desks.

The WL building was run-down and drab. Pencils, pencil sharpeners, notepads, and telex strips lay on old, heavy teakwood furniture. Many desks had typewriters and calculators with paper rolls. Here and there, a computer screen reminded me that we had actually entered a new era. But it looked like that era hadn't reached these offices yet. Just like entering a decedent's estate, it felt as though grief from the air disaster and ghosts of the bankruptcy court were still draped on the walls. Or was it a reflection of my own underlying sadness after leaving SAS after so many years?

No matter. My first thought was: what in the world have I done?

When they welcomed me on board with a bottle of exclusive Linie Aquavit that had crossed the equator eight times—which I knew was one of the prides of the shipping company and only reserved for a few—I couldn't manage more than conditional pleasure. Never had I greeted a new year feeling more uncertain.

2

OUT IN THE WORLD EARLY

The values instilled in us as children help shape us as adults. Not that a good value base and good experiences necessarily make you a better person than one who has had a more difficult start. The reverse can just as easily be true. But what we experience or miss out on during childhood is key to understanding why we are who we are—which qualities we should cultivate and which ones we should control.

One of my most basic insights as a leader is that you must know yourself in order to lead others. If you aren't aware of your problem areas when challenged and where others should absolutely keep their distance, you will create a persistent insecurity in your leadership. Insecure leaders create insecure employees unable to give their best.

I was born in 1946. The post–war peace euphoria had long since settled. Rebuilding Norway after five years of German occupation preceded by 20 years of economic crises was a difficult task, as peple soon discovered. The housing situation was unstable. The Germans had concentrated their building activity around facilities important for the war: bunkers, roads, railways, etc.

We were fortunate to live in a three-bedroom apartment in a residential area in Oslo. I was an only child and had my own little bedroom. Having a bathroom a half flight of stairs down from the entryway was luxury for a family of three, even though our standard of living was simple. But most others had the same standard, even in this upscale area of Oslo. And it was much better than the old, stinking "outhouses" that were still common in many apartment buildings.

After working in the Oslo municipality and being active in the resistance during the war, my dad had just been employed as the Norwegian purchasing manager at the newly founded SAS airlines. I know little about his "illegal" activities, but whatever he did, it must have been enough to force him into hiding at the beginning of the war: he was admitted to Dikemark Hospital as a psychiatric patient. As a result, the Germans and the Norwegian State Police left him alone. It was in the hospital that he met the woman who would become my mother. She was an educated nurse. They had a good relationship and were very happy with each other. I remember that they constantly joked about whether my father's admission to the hospital was a cover-up or genuine.

SAS was founded by Danish National Airline, Norwegian National Airline, and Swedish National Airline. The companies were mostly dormant during the war, except for some activity in Sweden, a neutral country. The original intent to merge the companies was to be able to operate flights from Scandinavia to the rest of Europe and the world. The company would also be responsible for the operation of domestic traffic in all three countries.

The head office was based in Stockholm. The main airport and technical base was in Copenhagen. In the beginning, the Oslo branch had no other corporate tasks beyond supplying Copenhagen with passengers who were on their way to other destinations. This suited the company at that time. One of the many reasons why the once-proud SAS continually finds itself a hair's breadth from failing as an independent company is probably because that same structure exists to this day, although the largest traffic is actually from Norway's main airport, Gardermoen. The voice of Norwegian passengers, then and now, could be heard to say: "When I need to go somewhere, I don't want to go to Copenhagen first."

At the end of the 1940s, most people didn't fly. Flying was reserved for the busiest business travelers. But even they had to put up with adapting to the airlines' available routes based on technical operating considerations. This was how the post–war business sector operated in most areas. People had lived on ration cards for five years, and rationing existed for all sorts of capital goods, such as cars. Demand exceeded supply. Vendors targeted the market based on previous history and blind faith in existing technical solutions and products. In such a market, even businesses that are behind the times can be successful.

Experience and history make good ballast but a poor compass to guide the future course of a company in a market where customers have the power, and where supply far exceeds demand. Look at Tandberg Radio Factory, Norwegian Data, Kodak, Nokia, Sony Ericsson, and many other companies which at the time and in different ways were in the forefront. They discovered—too late—that the top is only a position on the way, not a place where you can relax. At the top, the only road to take goes downhill unless you set new goals by applying that very same energy and freedom to act that you had on the way up. We call this "jumping the curve"—setting new goals while you're still on the way up. It's too late to get back on top after the downturn has begun. This was, in fact, a specific area of focus at WL.

This is well known in professional sports. Skating coach Hans Trygve Kristiansen, who trained Johan Olav Koss in the 1994 Lillehammer Olympics, has a motto: "A world champion is not something you are; it is something that you have been or can be." Alpine star Kjetil André Aamodt swore that it is always the case that "The next one is the best." The Finnish ski jumping coach Mika Kojonkoski, who from 2002–2004 transformed Norwegian ski jumpers into the world's best, said, "I know that I am never as good as I can be."

Many of my friends were jealous when I was able to go to work with my dad. Since I was an only child, it was easy for Dad to take me everywhere. And there were fewer safety regulations then. To this day, I can still smell the raw aviation fuel and exhaust when the big silver gray aircraft with their rumbling propeller engines took off and landed. If the wind came from a certain direction, the harsh smell that assaulted my nose would make me sick. Nevertheless, it was the smell of adventure. The first flight

I remember was on a Metropolitan to Rome. I was only six or seven years old.

Mom started working at the largest hospital in Oslo after the war, but I never went to work with her. I had spent enough time in the hospital and doctors' offices as a polio patient when I was 18 months old. For several years, I received daily orthopedic treatments. By the time I started school, my left leg worked the way it should. The only permanent damage I had was that it was a little shorter than the right leg, but not so much that I limped. The method the doctor used to treat my leg had been regarded as heretical, it turned out later, for only one reason: it was ahead of its time.

I'm sure it was also due to my father's views on childrearing. Following the recommendations of the doctor, he enrolled me in a sport that probably requires the greatest strength and best leg motor control: ski jumping. Against all odds, I won the first jumping competition that I entered—a small boys' slope in a park in Oslo. It was a great moment—one that gave me tremendous motivation to tackle larger ski jumping hills.

At the time, ski jumping was the nearest one could get to flying without motorized aids. Perhaps I could have gone further in the ski jumping sport if I had been more committed. To this day, I'm still very fascinated by ski jumping's magical possibilities, especially when athletes can jump more than 250 meters (275 yards). But when you consider my starting point, which could just as easily have ended in greatly reduced mobility, mastering the skill and the joy that I could actually participate in any of the sports and activities I wished was probably most important.

Because of his job, Dad also got a different perspective on the rest of the world. He could see how small Norway was so far up north and felt that it was beneficial to give his son a broader perspective on life. There were plenty of opportunities to fly SAS to all parts of the world for free— or almost free. But with short holidays, it was difficult for Mom and him to travel long distances as a family, even in the summer. My mother had apparently come to terms with that. She felt it was acceptable for me to stay home with my friends and spend a week here and a week there. Dad found another solution.

By the age of nine, I was sent out in the world on my own, more specifically to the home of a Norwegian and his American family that my father knew in California. I stayed there for two months, the whole summer vacation. That was the start of a long series of vacations abroad where I more or less lived with people who were distant acquaintances of my father but strangers to me. Before I was 18, I had spent several months in Germany, Japan, Brazil, South Africa, and Kenya.

I always traveled alone but was taken care of by the SAS crew. I rarely felt afraid or lost. These trips helped me learn to fend for myself, and I became quite independent—no matter where I was and how I felt. This was one of Dad's ulterior motives. At the same time he wanted to develop my social skills, so I had to learn to mix with people I didn't know. Dad knew that well-being is not the only prerequisite for learning. One must be challenged and perhaps even depressed at times in order to grow. These experiences would come in handy during my later studies and at the start of my professional career.

Another effect was that I realized I had improved at meeting new people and experiencing unknown places. It was as if the world shrank to a manageable size. People were people, no matter where they lived. I could thrive anywhere by adapting to local conditions. Of course, I had no idea at the time how important these experiences would become, especially the trips to Germany, the United States, and Japan.

Back then, few young people had the opportunity to travel, except for those who became sailors. Fortunately, it has become much more common today. I think that is one of the most important positive contributions to globalization. Instead of sitting at home on the couch and viewing the world via TV, one meets a lot of people in real life. This provides completely new perspectives of the world of which we all are a part.

Dad understood that. In addition, he felt I should learn to work. When I was only 14, he arranged for me a vacation and weekend job at the airport. No one objected to that. I was virtually born into SAS and worked at the jobs that needed to be done. I came to know "the big boys," who for me weren't the SAS bosses but "the guys on the shop floor." They were proud of the important work they did and of the company for which they worked. I believe this experience made me feel I always was in touch with all levels of the organization when I reached top management.

It's possible that I was a little too chummy with the guys at old Fornebu. When Dad heard that I signaled planes to their stopping places, drove and operated the tractor with the charging unit, and even sat in the cockpit and read off the instruments measuring how much fuel was being filled in the tanks, he put his foot down. The pilots may have known where and how to park the plane, and they surely would have discovered that there was too little power or fuel on board before they took off, but there was a limit to the responsibilities a young whelp should be given.

So I was transferred to the baggage handlers, who thought it was great to get someone on the team who was small. I could take the worst job—storing and retrieving luggage all the way down in the belly of the plane. I was also allowed to run the "toilet tractor"; it wasn't exactly high status among the baggage handlers to clean the planes' toilets. That didn't matter to me: I got to drive a car.

It wasn't long before I started working the baggage handlers' weekend shift. I went Friday after school and worked to midnight. I worked on Saturday from six in the morning to eleven in the evening. On Sunday, I also started at six but finished by three o'clock in the afternoon. Sometimes I was so tired that I fell asleep as soon as I got home and slept until Monday morning when I went to school. During vacations, the shifts could be longer and breaks shorter; there was almost no limit on how much we temps could work, as long as we kept awake and did the job as efficiently as possible. Even back then, both passengers and the company's management were concerned that the baggage was expedited quickly so the planes could come and go on schedule.

I earned enough money to buy my own clothes, extra sports equipment, and other things I wanted. I could also afford my own vacation trips during my free time. I even put some money in the bank. Earning my own money gave me a sense of freedom, and I'm sure it helped build up my independence. In reality, there was nothing exceptional in that. The general attitude in the 1960s was that one worked as much as one could.

Sailing was the second thing that gave me a sense of freedom. Several of my friends and I went on weekend and multi-week sailing voyages, where we slept in the cockpit under the cockpit tent and endured the conditions that came with it. Sailing taught us to trust in ourselves and in our abilities to read the wind and weather. Only then could we influence the voyage, whether in stormy or calm seas. We were a tight-knit bunch; in 1964, we started the GIFH Club (Guys in From the Sea). It still exists today: 17 close friends aged 68 to 70 years. I have traveled around the world my whole professional life, but this group has always been an important anchor in my life.

Perhaps my choices in life would have been different had Dad not sent me around the world before I realized the value of the trip. I was quite determined early in life that I would study abroad, and so I took a student trade course at Oslo Trade School in 1967 after getting my high school degree at Fagerborg School the previous year. My plan was to go to St. Gallen, Switzerland, where several of my good friends were studying economics. I decided to stay in Nuremberg instead of going to St. Gallen. Once more, my father's SAS contacts determined my choice, this time with a paper manufacturer in Nuremberg who could provide me a place to stay and a job to learn German as preparation for the admittance test and for my studies.

I arrived in Nuremberg in August 1967 and enrolled at the venerable Friedrich-Alexander University in a faculty equivalent to Business University College in Bergen. I thought my German proficient enough from previous stays and work in the German paper factory, but when I sat down in the large auditorium to follow the first lecture, I discovered that I barely understood the terminology.

Had I not been accustomed to managing on my own in the world, I would probably have become discouraged. Instead, I thought, "It's five years before I have to take the exam. I'm sure I'll learn the language by then. There have been plenty of Norwegians here before me who have accomplished it. In the meantime, I will try to make the most out of the situation and learn what I can. What matters here is taking one step at a time and trusting I will reach my goal on time."

3
WHAT I CAN DO SOMETHING ABOUT

Nuremberg is the second largest city in Bavaria after Munich. For many years, people connected it to the trials that took place there in 1946, when four judges on the Allied military court from the victorious nations—the United Kingdom, the United States, France, and the Soviet Union—handed down the death sentence to 12 German Nazi leaders who had not already been killed or committed suicide. Seven were sentenced to life imprisonment. Up until 1949, an American military court judged hundreds of Germans in subordinate levels under the same international law provisions: war crimes and crimes against humanity.

Obviously, I had heard of those trials, which took place during the first years of my life. But I had no other connection with them other than feeling those responsible for the war were justly punished. The Germans treated Norwegians kindly, just as I experienced with the family in the Rhineland. Even during the war, the Germans never considered Norwegian citizens as enemies: in the Germans' minds, they came as liberators. From their point of view, they had no unfinished business with us when they were forced to travel back to their devastated homeland.

We met many Germans who had been stationed in Norway during the war. This wasn't so strange because

Hitler had placed at least 300,000 soldiers in Norway to protect the war's important transport of ore and herring oil from Northern Norway. Most of them lived peacefully compared with those who fought on the Eastern and Western fronts. They often spoke warmly about our country. Some told me that they had met their great love in the North and had children in Norway. That was a bit more difficult to deal with. We knew exactly how Norwegians treated "Kraut children" and their mothers.

The nearly thousand-year-old Nuremberg was virtually razed to the ground during the war. Only the beautiful *Lorenzkirche* and parts of the city's proud historical symbol *Die Kaiserburg* were left standing. The castle ruins and the rest of the old city wall that had been destroyed were rebuilt by the time I came in 1967. The work was so good that it looked as if both the castle and town wall had been there all the time.

I knew there were a number of Norwegians in Nuremberg. On one of my first days, I sat alone in a coffee shop eating lunch and feeling a little lost. Two other young men sat a few tables away. When I heard them speaking Norwegian and realized they had been in town for a while, I went over to them. It was a smart move: they made me feel at home by introducing me to the rest of the Norwegian students and giving me a lot of good advice on how I could get the most out of my stay and studies.

The Norwegian students had a regular place for some lively carousing on Friday and Saturday nights—the Baumwolle. Southern Germans were very easygoing and tolerated rather large doses of Norwegian weekend binge drinking. The group I eventually became a part of had acquired some good habits that limited Friday's excesses: we were always at the reading room at 10 a.m. on Saturdays and read until late afternoon, followed by a few hours of football. Then we were ready for Baumwolle and Saturday's festivities.

Many German students and students from other European countries also followed this pattern. I quickly learned how sensible it was. Saturday was always a good day: We helped each other with technical questions that had cropped up during the course of the week, and the soccer ball reminded us that the head works best when attached to the body. In the beginning, I used quite a few of these Saturdays to help improve my German and gradually was able to keep up with the lectures.

For the first three months, I held a part-time job in a paper factory, which helped improve my German, but I realized that it was too much for me to work and at the same time maintain my studies. I was still able to hold on to a room in the home of my contact at the human resources department of the company. In practice, I had the entire townhouse, located way beyond the city limits, to myself. This arrangement lasted about a year; I then moved to a dorm room within walking distance of the university.

Unfortunately, some Norwegian students were overcome by Baumwolle and other temptations. They were so accustomed to the very rigid Norwegian drinking restrictions that they succumbed to the enticements offered by unlimited southern German nightlife and the freedom of student life. Some dropped out and did not graduate. Others came home with considerably heavier baggage: alcohol addiction.

Without ever realizing it, I think I had gained a relaxed relationship with alcohol during my childhood. There was little of it at home; I can't remember Mom or Dad being visibly intoxicated. Of course, as a minor, I was never served alcohol during my visits with families around the world. But on these trips, I noticed that people dealt with alcohol more openly than in Norway—without abusing it. Bottles stood openly in the living room, and beer or wine was normal with dinner. I noticed that one could even purchase liquor in regular shops. But hardly anyone got drunk. Wine was no more special than potatoes, except for the custom to toast with wine when it was on the dinner table.

Nuremberg was so pleasant that I soon thought, "What shall I actually do in St. Gallen? Perhaps the teaching was more modern there and the environment more international." By 1898, the University of St. Gallen had already established itself as a business academy. Then again, Friedrich-Alexander University in Nuremberg was a venerable institution of learning with many different faculties and was definitely much more conservative in every way. Sometimes one felt that the professors had been at the university since it was founded in 1742.

The environment, however, was very good. It was as if cultural, academic, and scientific values had somehow seeped into the walls. I remember that I always felt a certain awe when I stepped into *auditorium maximum* (the big lecture hall), as if learning and being a part of an almost 230-year-old educational institution was in itself a privilege.

When the student uprising started in Paris in May 1968 and quickly spread to the rest of Europe and North America, I thought that it would ignite in Nuremberg as well. But a rebellion didn't really take root. With our studies of law, medicine, science, or economics, there was never room for unrest with us.

Although the university stood out as old-fashioned, we concentrated on what we could do: obtain the best possible results. The older Norwegian students worked hard to encourage the younger Norwegian students to develop good study habits. There was a so-called "home senior" in the dorm across the street from the university, a kind of steward whose job was to look after students' interests with the management of the dorm. I was put forward as a candidate, ran an election campaign, and was elected. As a benefit, I was rewarded with a single room and could, in principle, stay at the dorm as long as I wanted.

I was also the leader of an event we called *Norwegerabend,* which was simply throwing a giant party for fellow students and professors to showcase Norwegian export products. The Norwegian Embassy, Association of Norwegian Students Abroad, and a number of Norwegian companies participated in the event.

These two tasks began my leadership experience. Even then, I discovered some of my strengths and weaknesses as a manager. I have had to work on these throughout my adult life. I was good at implementation and progress, and quite good at bringing intelligent people to my team. On the other hand, I had little patience with people who lacked the same capacity or pace as I. It often seemed easier to do things myself than to let others try. That is an unfortunate quality in a leader, but I paid it little heed at the time.

Even though I was basically goal oriented about everything I did and considered it fun sitting in the driver's seat, I never planned a leadership career. I always took one step at a time and tried to take advantage of any and all opportunities that came my way. This is a basic principle that I have followed throughout my adult life, and which I think is quite healthy and recommend.

Knowing that you have the prerequisites to master the challenges you encounter gives you peace of mind, even if the solutions aren't immediately obvious. The alternative to the above is chasing after jobs that look great based on position and money but where your qualifications do not fit the position's actual content. If you do that, you will be neither a good employee nor manager. The safest method reveals itself along the way. As long as you know who you are, where you are, and where you are going, you will arrive at your destination even though you may have to take a few detours. Only in geometry is the straight line the shortest path between two points.

When reflecting on goals and methods, sometimes it's necessary for a leader to go a little farther or to stop and take a few steps back so everyone on the team can be on the same page.

I acquired many good friends among the Norwegian students. However, I intentionally leaned toward being with the Germans when we had assignments so I could work with them, not only because of their facility with the language that I would later take the exam in and because of their thought processes, but also because of their good work discipline. Besides, they were downright pleasant and polite.

Angelika, who would later become my wife, also lived in the dorm. Her father had several textile agencies in which her mother also was heavily involved. In practice, they were at customers' beck and call 24/7. They could not take a break for fear their competitors would immediately fill the void. I decided never to be a textile agent or anything that required attending to customers all the time. How wrong I was. Little did I know then that consideration for customers wholly propelled the most demanding organizational processes I would later come to manage at both SAS and WL.

Did I perhaps receive a bit of good old-fashioned retail culture from my father-in-law after all? Customer orientation is far from a new concept; it just seems that way every time a company is more concerned with its own production and profit than with what customers actually want.

Spring of 1972 approached. A bit farther south, the Germans prepared for the Summer Olympic Games in Munich, the first on German soil since the infamous Berlin Olympics in 1936, which, unfortunately, people also remember for everything other than sport. We students were preparing for exams. Thanks to my relationship with Angelika, her family and friends, and my own German student circle, I spoke and wrote German fluently. I had stopped worrying about language over the last year and really enjoyed the feeling of being able to concentrate 100 percent on academics. Even the toughest texts came easily. My major was macroeconomics and business administration. As electives, I took marketing, communication, statistics, and corporate leadership.

Meanwhile, I continued working on my diploma thesis that would qualify me for *Diplomkaufmann*, the equivalent of a business degree. I chose a theme in the only subject area in which I had some professional experience: air transport. I still worked shifts as a baggage handler at Fornebu during the holidays, and it had occurred to me that there was little planning in how the airlines promoted and organized their cargo services in relation to free capacity on planes. Air cargo was still regarded as very marginal. Sometimes the planes were full of cargo; other times they were nearly empty.

Therefore, I took on a task where there was plentiful but poorly systematized source material. The title of the task was *Marktforschung für das Frachtaufkommen der Luftfahrtgesellschaften* (Market Research for the Development of Airfreight). It was an ambitious project, but I received great feedback both from the professor who was my supervisor and, later, from the SAS air cargo boss who had helped me with his professional input. My grade was not bad. The professor wanted me to continue as his scientific assistant while working on my doctorate degree.

I politely refused. I was impatient to get on with real life. Through a friend of Angelika's father, a bank executive, I expected a job in the marketing department of the Lufthansa catering company, Lufthansa Service. It was a newly created position in a new department, and I felt that the job was almost created for me. The condition was that I pass the exam.

I worked hard with a German study companion; we had become good friends both professionally and socially. We studied day and night because the final exam at the University of Nuremberg was no laughing matter. It consisted of written exams and, later, oral exams in the same subjects. The grades ranged from one to six, where one was the best. If you made five or six in one subject, you had to take all the subjects over again no matter how good the marks were in the other subjects. If you made three or better in all written subjects, you could not fail even if you did terribly in the oral. But if you made a four in a subject, you had to make a minimum of the same grade in the oral to keep from failing. If you failed in one subject, you had to take them all again.

I held my own in all of the subjects, except in macroeconomics, which I liked very much. Nevertheless, I bombed on the written exam, making only a four. It meant that I had to have a minimum of four in my oral. I made good grades in the other subjects so I did not need to worry too much. But they would not count if I failed my oral in macroeconomics.

The oral test was a strain on everyone, especially on those of us who depended on performance. The hearing was public—similar to a doctoral dissertation—and afforded great entertainment for fellow students and many of the city's citizens. The room was packed; people stood along the walls and laughter broke out when the candidates either could not answer the questions they were asked or answered incorrectly.

They called us in alphabetically; normally two would go in at the same time. For some reason, there was a delay. I remember standing in the hallway and waiting for a half hour while my nervousness increased. The night before, on the phone with Angelika, I had a little breakdown. I was probably not only nervous but also overworked after all the reading I had done during the last few weeks. For me, it was not just about the exam but also about a top job. We had even talked about marrying when I got a job.

Finally, there were only five of us left in the hall. Suddenly, all five of us were called in at the same time, and since S was the next letter, I was to be first. For some reason, though, the professor and his assistants reversed the order, so the last man, alphabetically, was tested first. He was asked many questions that I would not have stood

a chance of answering coherently. Yet this candidate ex-
celled and received the best grade. I would have breathed
a sigh of relief, but the nightmare was far from over. Candidate number two barely made it. Numbers three and
four failed; they could not answer a single question—to
the public's great amusement.

Then it was my turn. At this point, I think I was so
exhausted by the excitement that I was hardly afraid anymore. Suddenly my prospective slayer, the professor,
asked if I could give a quick explanation of Keynes' theo-
ries. I jumped and could not believe my ears. This was a
subject I knew a lot about; the answers just tumbled out
of me, undoubtedly rather incoherent and inelegant, but
I had a feeling that the content held and I probably had
come through the eye of the needle.

We waited an hour before receiving our grades. It
was a beautiful spring day in Nuremberg, but I remember
nothing else during that hour. I stood patiently and waited with the other candidates. It was my first oral exam;
I knew that if I passed this, I could soon say goodbye to
school for good. I could do very badly on the other orals in
the other subjects and still get my diploma.

The grade came: I made a two. I cheered and went
straight down to Hauptmarkt Square and sat alone at a
sidewalk restaurant where I ordered two beers at once
"to be sure." I emptied the first one quickly. I took my
time with the other and thought about life. I was *Diplomkaufmann*. I had a job at Lufthansa. The alternative was
that I had to study another year.

But the best thing of all—which was worth one more beer—was that Angelika and I could be married.

I was 25 years old and had done my best. I had a diploma from a renowned German university and permanent employment in an exciting job at one of the world's major airlines.

When Angelika and I honeymooned through Switzerland and Austria in her red Beetle, I realized that it was the first long summer holiday I had taken since I started high school. I remember enjoying every minute: I was happy and I felt I deserved it.

4
REAL LIFE

On August 1, 1972, dressed in a dark suit with a white shirt and tie, I sat in my own office at the Lufthansa base in Frankfurt where the subsidiary Lufthansa Service main office was located. I was employed in the marketing department of the company; a year later, I was appointed to marketing manager. The company ran catering services and restaurants within the Lufthansa system. It was my first real job—*position* is probably a more accurate word.

The boss I reported to was in charge of the entire company. The only meeting I had with him, when he hired me, took so little time that I hardly dared to believe he was serious. The entire employment interview consisted of a short conversation where he simultaneously browsed quickly through my diploma thesis and asked a few questions about what I had done before and during my time in Nuremberg. Then he explained the position and asked if I thought I had the necessary qualifications and motivation for the job.

The marketing department was established because someone thought it necessary to improve and expand the Lufthansa Service company. There were many new business opportunities with other airlines and airports abroad where Lufthansa flew a large number of German passengers. Germans are like Norwegians: they want to be served what they are accustomed to no matter where they are in the world, whether on the ground or in the air. Since the department was new, I would be its first and only employee. Eventually, I had an executive title. In the beginning, though, I had functional responsibility only, no staff.

I felt the job hit the mark. It was possible to both safeguard and further develop already-established good ideas and come up with new things. With my abilities, this was about as close as I could get to a dream job, which I expressed to the boss. The answer he gave me was that nothing more was necessary for me to be employed except to pass my final exam. He had not been worried at all. Had he only known . . . .

I said nothing about how close I had been to retaking the entire exam, but asked if there were going to be more interviews beyond the standard tests that Lufthansa ran on all of their job candidates. That was not necessary, he said. The bank executive had assured him that I was a reliable person and I certainly would do a good job.

I never forgot this. Through the years, I hired many people. I tried all the interview methods, psychological tests, and recruitment experts. The only time I made a serious mistake was when I let them override my gut instinct. Often I did not need any more information than my old Lufthansa boss had to be sure I had found the right person. A firm handshake. A clear look. A joke and a smile at the right moment. These are testimonials and references that are not tactically positioned but speak for themselves. Last but not least: that the person can give a clear picture of what he or she can and wants to accomplish.

All of this tells me a lot more than whether the candidate has this or that psychological profile, which I can plot into this or that matrix like a DNA test. Such clear gut information can, of course, supplement a picture and may well tip the scale if one is in doubt or has no clear intuitive feeling about the person. But then again, perhaps one should not hire that person.

Hiring people that you do not know is one of the difficult—and potentially expensive—tasks a corporate leader must deal with. One incorrect hire can be enough to disturb the balance of an entire management team or can result in the business losing momentum in a crucial area. It does not have to mean that the person is incompetent but that he or she does not fit into the job. No matter what tools and intuition I used, I also made some unfortunate hiring decisions.

Similarly, a good hiring decision can make more pieces fall into place than just the one person and that person's area of responsibility because he or she also energizes others and/or increases the degree of interaction between individuals and departments. This is the ideal scenario. Fortunately, I experienced it several times, both with employees and contracted consultants. Unfortunately, I also experienced the opposite, most often because of the times I failed to rely on my intuition.

The heart of Lufthansa Service was actually a huge kitchen the company operated in Frankfurt. The kitchen distributed food to planes, restaurants, and other catering establishments, cooked to the desired degree of skill, packed, and supplemented with the right drinks. It was a tireless and very impressive exercise in logistics. Much of the food was fresh, which had to come in and go out on the same day. I remember initially spending quite a bit of time getting to know all the systems and the flow in the deliveries.

The head of the LSG wrote a book on leadership. It was called *Wir da oben, Ihr da unten* (*We Up Here, You Down There*, 1973). Both the book's title and leading principles taught me a lot about how not to lead. The thinking was based on the old hierarchical model that characterized the management philosophy of the time, and concentrated on the importance of responsibility and reporting. By itself, that is a virtue of necessity in all organizations. However, the book's recipe for *how* one convinces *"Ihr da unten"* (You down there) to accept the necessary responsibility and report correctly was somewhat out of date. This was no longer acceptable even in Germany, one of the European countries in which autocratic management by giving orders and disciplinary exercises had survived the longest.

The typical German leadership was undergoing an upheaval. The country was located—and still divided—between the Soviet dictatorship and Western democracies. When you considered the conditions in West Germany and East Germany, it was not difficult to see which form of government had promoted the highest growth and most satisfied citizens. Many leaders intuitively drew the conclusion that both citizens and employees who have a part in determining development are more satisfied and perform better than those who have requirements and solutions come from the top down.

Meanwhile, Lufthansa became just as much of an international company as it was a national company. People at all levels had received numerous ideas elsewhere. This was a little background for growth opportunities for the catering company where I was going to work. In reality, the popular leadership style was considerably more modern than this book suggests. It was also the boss's own management style. I was given a lot of freedom to perform my job my way. With the clear goal of strengthening our position and developing new business opportunities and areas for the company, I could start anywhere.

I did not see much of my boss even though I formally reported to him. As CEO, he was constantly on the road. One of my main supporters was his assistant, with whom I gained a very good relationship and who had invaluable expertise.

He had grown up in Berlin, was a trained chef, and was a few years older than I. When I began work, he was busy directing preparations for the company's catering involvement in the Summer Olympic Games in Munich. The games were to begin on August 26, and Lufthansa had not only sponsored flight tickets and freight, but also wanted to use the games to highlight the capabilities of Lufthansa Service.

This was a great opportunity for me to familiarize myself with all of the company's services and how to market them. I realized the line of thinking was also that we would use part of the engagement later to promote Lufthansa's catering and service business.

On September 5, the terrorist group Black September put a brutal and tragic stop to all plans. Eight Palestinian terrorists stole into the Olympic Village, killed two Israeli athletes, and took nine hostages. The only thing the world associated with the otherwise well-arranged Olympics in Munich in 1972 was, of course, the terrorists' actions. We could not use any of what we had contributed as an external reference when we went out to sell our services. Nonetheless, within the company there was a lot to learn. Owing to the violent activities of the Baader–Meinhof Gang, or *Rote Armee Fraktion* as they called themselves, Lufthansa also had to learn to live with terror on German soil and to take precautions. With the fierce attack on the peaceful Olympic camp in Munich, emergency and security work had to be upsized and intensified—so, too, within our part of the business.

The market and professional lesson for us was learning to adapt deliveries to the nation's differing customs and preferences, and to bring this in sync with our own logistics. If you are to supply a plane that flies from Frankfurt to Istanbul with food and drink, you need to be able to offer European, Muslim, and Jewish fare. If you are good at it, the likelihood increases that you will also supply the Lufthansa aircraft and other aircraft on the way back. If this activity increases, at some point it will pay to establish a kitchen in Istanbul. Even though you maintain the same standard, the prices will be lower. Then you will be competitive with other airlines that have the same needs for different fares on the same and corresponding air routes. Also, once you have a kitchen connected to the airport, you can open a restaurant that satisfies the same customer groups. Yes, perhaps you can even gain deliveries to hotels and restaurants where the airline passengers stay.

This line of thinking showed the potential we had in the market. I went to Istanbul, Lima, Rio, Sao Paulo, and a number of other global Lufthansa destinations looking for opportunities to expand catering for Lufthansa and other international airlines. The main criteria for choice of destination were heavy international traffic and potential for growth.

We discovered early that it was easier to get a foothold if local participants were on the owner's side. One deal after another fell into place. I was young and highly motivated. Angelika and I rented an apartment in Sulzbach am Main, not far from her parents, and I looked forward to going to work each day. Angelika worked as a teacher at the local school.

Occasionally I met friends from Norway, but most of my time was focused on work and home. Working at Lufthansa was very inspiring—mainly because I was successful and in tune with my assignments. I traveled around the world with blind faith in what I did. It was almost as though there were no restrictions. I felt at home wherever I went and seldom heard "no" when trying to schedule a meeting.

In retrospect, I think I always felt comfortable because I was so used to adapting to new places. It always seemed good enough to just be who I was while showing respect for the specific culture of those I met, whether they were from Europe or from another continent. It was as though I only needed to trust that I would do the right things—without pretending. Like when my father sent me off to the other side of the world when I was still a child, and I was never afraid. Like when I tried to follow the first lecture in the *auditorium maximum* in Nuremberg and did not feel lost.

Perhaps we call it self-reliance, a combination of confidence and humility both with yourself and your surroundings. Without humility, confidence can quickly transform itself into hubris and complacency. If humility gets the upper hand, one is quickly put on the defensive and becomes unsure and fearful.

The deals were not always a piece of cake. Yet, as long as I knew we had done our best, I never considered a deal that was unsuccessful as a defeat. So I was never angry or upset; most of the time, I left a potential customer or partner with the feeling that the door was still open. When new possibilities or changes occurred that indicated a new situation, it was easy to get in touch with them again. If you show everyone the same respect and behave appropriately, you never need to be afraid to look at yourself in the mirror.

After a few years, the business became so extensive that we had to hire more staff. At a mere 27 years old, I was now the formal head of the marketing department and a member of the management group at Lufthansa Service. Also, I was the manager of a so-called *Beirat*, an advisory board with the purpose of supporting all parts of the business both in terms of opening doors to new customers, suppliers, and business partners, and in strengthening the business relationships we already had.

Eventually the responsibility for strategic purchases was moved to the marketing operation. This was one side of the catering company's operation that had not been systematically worked with, but to some extent it involved what we marketed. The volume of tenderloin, for example, was up to several tons per week.

Through a restaurant chain, we contacted a German living in Argentina. He was married to the sister of the old industry giant Alfred Krupp, who played a key role during the escalation of the German war machine in the 1930s and 1940s, but no one cared about that anymore. He owned one of the largest ranches in Argentina with herds of cattle and a capacity to deliver meat in large quantities at a good price. Together with a chef from our main kitchen, I traveled to Argentina to meet him.

Many Germans had emigrated from Germany to South America and were successful in various types of business. Our man had built up a huge *estancia* (ranch). The property was so enormous that we had to fly from one end to the other in order to see it all in the time we had at our disposal. First, we toured a large slaughterhouse in Cordoba; afterward, a private plane flew us to the ranch.

We were treated very well. The chef gave approval, and after negotiating the price and other terms for delivery, we ended up importing two tons of Argentine tenderloin per week, mainly served in first class.

It was at Lufthansa where I first learned the many different ways to give full-paying passengers a sense that they were getting extra value for their full-fare tickets. This was the same kind of thinking behind what made SAS a success throughout the 1980s, particularly when we introduced and began to cultivate "The Businessman's Airline."

My dad still worked for SAS. He was happy that I was starting my career in the airline industry, but felt that I would have greater developmental opportunities at SAS. I didn't think that much about it. I thought I advanced all the time at Lufthansa, where I worked on almost all of the projects I wanted. We went so far that we even developed a resort in Bavaria. But then we began to reach a limit as to how much space there was under the wings of an airline at that time.

In the 1970s, airlines had no specific strategy for developing and owning hotels. Their task was generating flights and serving passengers en route to and from airports. When a number of airlines, including SAS, later became shareholders in hotel chains, it became an immediate success. That way, they had influence over even more of the passenger's overall trip and were able to offer total packages, which increased both revenue and loyalty of each passenger.

One day my father sent me a job posting from SAS. The company was looking for management trainees who had solid education at the bottom and who were willing to go from apprentices to management. The job at Lufthansa was still exciting. However, I began to have the desire for new challenges and wanted to move north.

SAS was looking for five management trainees, two from Norway, two from Sweden, and one from Denmark. The company had developed a comprehensive management trainee program. Trainees would first learn all the ins and outs of the company, from the front customer counter with ticket sales, booking, check-in, station services, cargo sales and handling, and so on—and how the whole company was organized from bottom to top. Candidates would then find an area within the business where they could develop their leadership capabilities.

I applied and was lucky enough to get a first interview. It reminded me very little of that first targeted recruitment call two and a half years earlier. I still remember the first question in the SAS recruitment process: What do you think about yourself?

How could I answer? That I was a brilliant candidate with many good qualities and skills far above average? That I was a mediocre young man with poor self-esteem and a need for new challenges? I felt that these general questions were meaningless. I thought, at that time, it was not what kind of self-esteem one has that matters in business. What was important is what one has done, what one thinks one can do, and, last but not least, how one will do it. *Don't tell — show!*

Many self-images are pure wishful thinking, based solely on one's successes after omitting all the inevitable setbacks one has if one is trying to accomplish something at all. That self-image is a glossy photo. Some have a correspondingly poor self-image that becomes even more inadequate because they compare it with others' seeming successes.

Despite this, the possessors of either of these self-images can be excellent employees, but that requires that they are seen, measured, rewarded, and guided by what they actually accomplish in terms of goals and expectations, and not by what they or others think or believe they are. Only then, when one begins to see patterns in what one does and does not do and what connection it has with achieved results, can one begin to approach a realistic self-image.

I don't remember my answers to what I felt were meaningless questions. I'm sure it had something to do with the fact that I was happy with any accomplishment in my job at Lufthansa and that I had learned a lot but that I was ready for new challenges. My answers obviously contained some of what he wanted to hear because I advanced to the next round of interviews with several of the top bosses at SAS. It was then that I began to really want the job. My competitive instincts had probably also been awakened when I learned that I was one of 600 Norwegian applicants who were about to get one of the two trainee positions and that the other candidate was most likely internal.

I felt I had won a world championship when I was told that I was the one external applicant who had made it through. However, I had to take a sharp decrease in salary. All the travel would mean only a few hours at home with my family (our first son, Jørgen, was just a year old). For eight months I spent the whole week, Sunday evenings to Friday evenings, in Copenhagen and then later in Stockholm.

When I started at SAS School in Copenhagen on February 1, 1975, I began my weekly commute to my family in Germany. Sometimes I did not come home before Saturday morning and had to leave early Sunday because there was no available seat on the aircraft. (Seats were given to passengers and SAS employees who were at higher levels in the company before they were given to trainees.) I soon realized that my SAS journey would be longer and tougher than the one I had gone through at Lufthansa. On the other hand, it would probably bring new, exciting assignments.

5
APPRENTICE

We were five young men staying at the Hotel Globetrotter in Copenhagen and participating in a fantastic program. I believe, in principle, that afterward we could have run any division of SAS. At the same time, we had a lot of fun and developed friendships that continued later as well, both on the job and off.

In the late fall, we completed our apprenticeship in Copenhagen and moved to the Stockholm headquarters. Through SAS, I was offered an apartment in the suburb of Råsunda so the family could move. It suited our meager budget, but we all hated the thought of living there, especially when Angelika had no job and would be alone with our young son in the immense concrete desert that Råsunda truly was.

Fortunately, we were able to borrow some money to buy a townhouse in Ekerö, a green island at Lake Mälaren outside of Stockholm. Some other SAS employees also lived there, and we gradually began to socialize with them. Occasionally, though, it was lonely for a German woman in Stockholm, although Angelika had learned some Norwegian during our several vacations in Norway.

Outwardly, the little Skaug family appeared well off. We drove a sturdy BMW purchased in Germany after selling Angelika's Beetle. I worked at SAS, one of the elite jobs at the time. Even so, our finances were tight and we had to monitor our spending to keep within our budget.

It was not much fun for Angelika, but for me, who had never had to worry about having enough money for what I wanted since I was a teenager, it was a good lesson. Also, it was a good test of what I was willing to sacrifice in order to move up. One must be willing to make sacrifices to achieve something different and better. I could probably have gotten a different and much better paying job if I had tried but not nearly with the same growth opportunities that SAS was offering at that time.

Still, it was great when the family was together; we were good at finding fun things to do. We had a passion for life and found out that it was better to make the best of a situation rather than sit around and mope. We concentrated more on the opportunities we had and less on the limitations, and that made us more enjoyable company. Angelika found a good friend who was also a stay-at-home mother with young children. It turned out later that the house was a good investment. During the two years we lived there, its value tripled. That possibility had not even occurred to us back then.

My first job at SAS was in the cargo department. The boss had read my diploma thesis from Nuremberg and thought I would be of most use there. The job was straightforward and important enough, consisting mainly of a number of projects. It was interesting to get a practical approach and delve even deeper into the issues I had discussed in my thesis. It became evident, though, that there was a slight cultural difference between those who worked with freight and those who worked with passengers. Filling planes with people seemed more honorable than filling them with boxes and containers. Air cargo was, in a way, in its infancy and did not enjoy the same priority. Perhaps that was the underlying factor for such poor business development in this area, as I had come to realize through my thesis.

Flying was still uncommon for most people. A plane trip was something one talked about with neighbors and friends, perhaps because airline prices were high compared to trains and buses. The market for business travelers was going through a small recession due to a global crisis in shipping, oil, and industry. Both SAS and the other European airlines struggled with profitability. The airline industry was not particularly flexible or innovative. Very few of the airlines were prepared for the new competitive situation that came about due to deregulation of the airline market throughout the 1980s, which resulted in a number of new, lower-cost airlines.

In Norway, SAS competed with Braathens SAFE. The main competitor for domestic traffic in Sweden was Linjeflyg (which SAS purchased in 1993, just as SAS eventually took over Braathens SAFE in Norway). There was relatively little domestic traffic in Denmark because the distances are small. The international grid to SAS was designed to send most of the traffic via Kastrup Airport in Copenhagen. That was the most practical way to run SAS from a production standpoint. The passengers had to tolerate it, even if it meant unnecessary stopovers and long detours. The prevailing attitude was that you should consider yourself fortunate if you could travel by plane. As a trainee, there was not much I could do about it. Neither was I as concerned about passenger traffic. I thought freight was exciting enough because there was a lot to accomplish.

My next challenge as a trainee was sales. I was sent to the SAS office in Chicago to learn how to sell airline tickets. The job involved trials that even experienced salesmen probably would have turned down. From a family perspective, the move to Chicago and the United States went well. It represented something new and exciting; the family felt it was beginning to get rather quiet in Ekerö.

Some of my old friends from Fagerborg and Nuremberg thought I was quite fortunate. They predicted a bright career for me in the company. Not many were sent to the United States to work during that time. Even I had certain expectations, but any glamorous images I had about "the promised land" were soon laid to rest.

Before I knew it, I found myself sitting in a virtually empty house in a residential neighborhood in the suburbs of Chicago. The inventory consisted of a bed, a table, and two old chairs. There were no lights, so I had to use candles. Fortunately, I had a lighter and a low-quality battery radio. It looked like a toy gun and was a gift my father had received as a giveaway. I brought it almost as a precaution, not expecting it would be my only companion during my first few weeks in Chicago until my family joined me.

The only things I received at the SAS office in the city were a map of Chicago, a list of travel agents that I was to visit, and some SAS brochures. The message from the—to put it mildly—not quite charming Dutch manager to whom I reported was short and sweet: "Here you go. This is what you will work on. We have sales meetings every other Friday where you will report your results. Between meetings, we do not need to see you because you will be with customers."

I was thrown out of the first travel agency I visited Monday morning. I had the same result with the next one, although they greeted me with a little more respect. Some were pleasant, but there was little or no business. It turned out that the list I had received was not even closely representative. Many on the list did not even have customers who traveled to Europe.

After a few weeks, I began to hate getting up in the morning. I virtually had to drag myself out of bed. When I finally did get up, it would just be to visit more companies in the area to obtain more nos. Or perhaps some nice yeses or maybes, but minimal business. I saw no trace of that country where, with even a modest starting point, one could create an overnight success, so to speak.

I found no help from the Chicago office. The others had problems of their own. I had to figure it out by myself. I could not report any special results at the first few Friday meetings; I sold a few trips here and there but no deals, which was what I was supposed to get from the list.

At this point, I was feeling like I did after the first lecture at the University of Nuremberg when I understood nothing. I thought more and more often: this is a total flop! At least there was a difference in Nuremberg. I knew immediately what I had to do: I had to learn better German. In Chicago, I had no idea where to start.

One night I came home after a bad day at work. It was as unpleasant as in the beginning. I had no money to pay for lamps or furnishings because I wouldn't get the so-called accommodation allowance before Angelika and little Jørgen came and we were a family again. I lit the candles and turned on the radio. Some sentimental pop songs were playing, which fit perfectly with my mood. After a few beers, I soon sank deeper in self-pity than I've ever been.

My thoughts revolved around my deplorable situation. Here I am sitting alone, without my family and with nothing to take my mind off work except an old car that has to visit the repair shop once a week. I have a lousy boss who only makes demands and hasn't followed up with me once. My colleagues can't be bothered. Maybe they find delight in "the spy from Stockholm" who can't get a damn thing done. Now I understood why they wouldn't even try it but would rather send in a greenhorn from Scandinavia. This is like selling sand in the Sahara. It's a lost cause no matter what I do. I might as well throw in the towel and go home. There must be somewhere else they can use me other than this botched venture, this miserable undertaking.

If I had not been accustomed to challenging situations during my travels as a child, I probably would have bought a return ticket the next day. But something held me back. Perhaps it was these types of situations my dad had contemplated when he sent me around the world to various acquaintances where there were never any guarantees of thriving. Then I had to endure, whether I wanted to or not. And wasn't the real experience that things always work out—if one lives *with* the situation and does not waste energy on things one can do nothing about. I had experienced that in Lufthansa when I had been pretty much left to myself in the beginning. There had to be some solution to this hopeless situation too!

When the vicious cycle with the boss, colleagues, and travel agents had gone round and round for an endlessly long time, I got an inkling that there was something missing. All of a sudden, it struck me as clearly as one can only see things when on the brink of breakdown: customers! I had not met the customers yet! I was told that I was to sell SAS deals to travel agents. But who really travels with the airlines? Not the agents. They only sell the tickets. The customers buy them! Customers! Maybe they're just as disgruntled with the travel agencies as I am, even though I'm on the other side of the fence.

Customers! It was as if it sang inside of me. In that instant, I knew I had the solution! It was right in front of my nose. I just hadn't seen it because I had been more concerned with looking at my own miserable situation and inner strife rather than directing my sight outward.

During the next few days, I did a quick survey and found that a number of large companies in Chicago and in my sales territory had Europe as their main export market. That implied that they had to travel a lot along SAS routes. Yet none of them had agreements with SAS. It was quite possible to create my own key customer agreements with specific airlines and still let travel agents place the actual ticket orders. As a supplier, we could integrate and customize more service items than travel agencies could. But that meant going directly to the customers, not through travel agents.

That's what I did. Results occurred immediately. Soon I had established agreements with several major customers in my district in Chicago—companies such as the food giant Kraft, some of the big breweries, and outboard engine manufacturers Johnson and Evinrude, who oddly enough were next door to each other on Lake Michigan.

When travel agents discovered this, all of a sudden they wanted to talk with *me*. From a young punk who had about as little to offer as a beggar, I had now become an interesting collaborator with whom it was important to keep in touch. Major customers did not just travel to Europe: they were probably ripe for framework agreements with other airlines to other parts of the world as well. The travel agencies wanted a piece of that cake.

When we later began to develop group travel where travel agents could buy cheaper tickets for their customers, they were even more disposed to be friendly. It was like having found the right end of a rope in a jumbled mess.

Suddenly everything loosened. From being ready to give up, I had moved to thoroughly enjoying the job. Those horrible Friday meetings, where I always sat as inconspicuously as possible, became a delight. Not that I gloated when I sat with a considerably more visible posture. But in the sheer joy of finally achieving success, I didn't exactly place my light under a basket either, especially when some of the agreements I brokered were brought out as shining examples of good business.

You should be allowed to enjoy your results, as long as you don't create them at someone else's expense or lose the ability to enjoy others' success. You are not necessarily haughty when you enjoy your achievements, especially if you remember that you can always improve.

At this time Angelika and Jørgen joined me in the United States. I had missed them tremendously but was glad that they had not been there when things were at their roughest. Having a live wailing wall at home when you fall flat on the job may be helpful for a while, but before you know it, you pull your partner down with you. Then it is even more difficult to get up again.

Soon I received the accommodation allowance. Finally, there was contentment and well-being at home. Instead of discussing problems, we talked about new challenges and solutions. Angelika thought it was fun to help with what I was doing and had lots of good ideas. Who else travels—or is likely to travel—to northern Europe and Scandinavia? It has to be the descendants of the early Scandinavian immigrants. After a while, we met several of them and discovered that they were quite nostalgic. Of course, they would rather fly with a company from their ancestral homeland than any American airline. Exactly!

From the SAS office in Chicago, I could eventually operate in several states where I easily set up meetings with various Scandinavian immigrant associations. I had created a presentation that played on their basic homesickness and showed tourist films of Norwegian fjords, the Swedish archipelago, and Danish farmhouse vacations, etc. It didn't take long before ticket orders poured in.

It was insanely exciting and extremely enjoyable. A few months later, our second son, Christian, was born. Even though I was often on the road, I still felt that I had time to have a real family life. When we visited the Scandinavian communities, occasionally all four of us could go. No one thought it unusual that a young man from SAS took his family on tour.

In some of these communities, they created their own events with Scandinavian cuisine. We benefited from heartwarming hospitality. I had the feeling that they saw us more as saviors coming from their home country than as what we really were: salespeople. In the United States, by the way, there is no comparison. A salesperson is one who both helps the customer to become conscious of what he or she needs and then meets those needs. A commercial merchant can be regarded as a greater blessing than a charitable benefactor.

The positive results in Chicago resulted in my eventually receiving responsibility for Iowa, Nebraska, and

South Dakota. Soon I operated throughout the whole Midwest and made agreements with production companies, insurance companies, organizations, tour operators, and travel agencies. I no longer reported to the sales manager of the SAS office in Chicago (who eventually was helped to find a new job) but to the considerably more supportive district manager of central America, whose area stretched from Canada in the North to Venezuela in the South, and from New Orleans in the East to Texas in the West.

I knew that SAS and our three owner countries occupied a very good position as an airline. In the United States, we were competitive on price, had on-time departures and service, and had that extra connection to the ancestral homeland. Even among Jewish customers we had a little gold star, probably because of our role in the United Nations during the creation of the State of Israel in 1948. We flew them in SAS planes to Copenhagen where they connected to Tel Aviv, Israel, with either ours or other aircraft.

But with passengers from many more cities in the United States, it became increasingly obvious that the SAS grid had not adapted to the international traffic pattern. While the major American and European airlines created direct flights from several of the largest US cities to the major European capitals, SAS still reasoned the same way they did in Scandinavia. Most international traffic would pass through a major hub airport: Kastrup in Copenhagen.

SAS tried to make most of the traffic to Europe fly from Chicago via Montreal or from Los Angeles via Seattle to Copenhagen and then move on to the other Scandinavian cities and the rest of Europe. Our competition flew directly from the major US cities to several destinations in Europe.

After 18 months, we moved to New York where one of my main tasks was to examine how the grid was drawn up, both in terms of passengers and freight. I discovered quickly that a lot of changes had to be made if we were ever to sustain and expand the position we had created in the American market. Instead of the typical major airport thinking that all traffic should be routed via some large airports, we needed to create more direct flights both ways. It did not help that the airline hubs might be in the right place for the company when viewed from an operationally technical viewpoint if they were no longer optimal in relation to the market and passengers' wishes.

During this work, I met the newly appointed CEO of SAS, Janne Carlzon, several times. He wanted me in a five-man group that would be the driver for what was to be the biggest turnaround in SAS. The first thing we did was to orient the organization toward the market and adapt it to the passengers' travel patterns. Then we introduced new financial management systems that made it easier to measure the profitability of each route. Passengers and freight would no longer be measured in numbers and kilos, but in earnings, costs, and profits per kilometer for the different routes. This resulted in many eye-opening experiences and led to a restructuring of the route programs.

The job in New York was an even better position for gaining insight into both American and international aviation. I could not help but promote my views on where SAS stood in relation to what I saw of the competition, both in terms of product development, logistics, and market orientation. That was probably one of the reasons I was called back to the main office in Stockholm after about 18 months, where I was given the choice of one of two jobs: marketing manager or head of administration for intercontinental routes. I chose the second since it looked like the greatest opportunity for development for both the company and me.

The job change did not happen with my family's blessings. The time was 1981, and during our stay in the United States we had another son, Helge. Angelika remained in New York with the boys for eight months. We always tried to let the boys complete the entire school year. For me personally, it might not have mattered as much. I was on the road now almost all the time. My formal apprenticeship was over. Fortunately, the trip for work often went to New York, but there was little family life.

Even though the first few months of the apprenticeship in Chicago might have been absolute hell for an ambitious young man, in hindsight I regard it as one of the most valuable lessons I learned during my trainee period at SAS. Up until then, I had encountered mostly good fortune. But when I met with a trial, one which seemed so extreme that I even began to doubt myself and my abilities, I learned an important lesson about life: there is always a solution if you're willing to suffer a little while looking for it.

6

TEAR DOWN THE PYRAMIDS!

In late 1979, SAS hired Janne Carlzon after he achieved two successful turnarounds at Vingresor and Linjeflyg. At that point, it looked like SAS was going to show its first deficit in 18 years. Former management could see the party was almost over but was unable to implement necessary measures in time to adapt the company to the new competitive situation, nationally or international-ly. Among other things, one of those who had made the situation for SAS difficult in Sweden was Carlzon, who had "stolen" quite a bit of domestic traffic by filling up Linjeflyg's low-cost routes with passengers—and had achieved amazing profitability.

Bjørn Kjos achieved about the same in Norway with his new Norwegian company when he took SAS by sur-prise 25 years later, albeit from a slightly different starting point. However, that is another story we will come back to.

SAS had not managed to adapt to low-cost competi-tion and struggled with making other parts of the compa-ny profitable. You can read Carlzon's own description of the situation at SAS when he took over responsibility in his book, *Moments of Truth* (1985):

As a consequence of the so-called oil crises, the market for air transport had stagnated in the seventies, when it came to both passengers and cargo. SAS reacted in its customary fashion: cost cutting. One assumed that one had a fixed revenue, so one sliced expenses in accord with the cheese cutter principle—by reducing distributions of funds, much as with the national budget.

During this process, things our customers appreciated and were willing to pay for disappeared—while other things our customers were not interested in were kept. The company cut things in such a way that it negatively affected competitiveness; hence, market shares went down.

The internal effect was equally serious. The general rules took initiative away from coworkers and made them passive. In the end, no one felt responsible for costs.

Both managers and employees lacked crisis understanding. Few were accustomed to taking responsibility for their situation, not only because everyone had been used to things going well, but because of a top-heavy and controlling management. Overall understanding was correspondingly low. Cost cutting had come down as a directive, not as something for which the individual understood the necessity. Personnel had not been involved in coming up with ideas as to where reasonable cuts could be made, for example. Thus, grumbling began in the ranks, which filtered all the way down to customers.

During the transition from cartel to competition, SAS lost important market shares. People experienced decreased service. Kastrup remained the main airport for SAS, but it had a poor reputation. Meanwhile, many noted that the company had overcapacity on many routes.

Since the concensus was that costs had already been cut to the bone using traditional methods, the only way to improve profitability was to increase revenues—without increasing expenses. If the company was to regain share in a stagnant market, there was only one thing to do: SAS would have to find new ways to let passengers know that they received more for their money when they traveled with SAS. In practice, that meant improving service.

By 1980–81, SAS had carved out its new strategy. In the course of a three-year plan, SAS would be "the best airline for business travelers who travel frequently." The strategy was not surprising; all airlines try to flirt with full-paying business travelers to achieve the best possible margin. But the way this was done remains one of the most effective turnarounds in which I took part—except that we forgot something very significant that would often later come up.

The organization was divided into separate business areas. We created "route sectors" to monitor those that made money and those that didn't and which needed special measures put in place. The sectors included intercontinental routes; European routes; domestic routes in Norway, Sweden, and Denmark; as well as cargo. This was a decisive plan. It was not enough to change financial management systems if lines of reporting weren't changed so that the responsibility was well defined.

The most visible change for passengers was the creation of a new business class for European routes: Euro-Class. On long-haul routes, we abolished the traditional first class. Used mostly by the company's directors, it was jokingly called "the most expensive directors' canteen in the world," and some of them protested the change. Instead, business class was upgraded to a cross between the old first class and business class, called first business class, while tourist class remained about the same.

In practice, the greatest market impact on long-haul routes was the creation of several new direct routes between Scandinavia and major cities in Europe, the United States, and the Far East. Thus, the routes were adapted to businessmen's travel patterns. They wanted the fewest possible plane changes so they could either work or sleep with the least number of interruptions. SAS purchased several smaller aircraft, Boeing 767s, to make the long-distance route more flexible than with the big Boeing 747s. We handed South American and African traffic over to other airlines. Air traffic requires a large support system on the ground; SAS did not have that in these parts of the world.

We dropped the big A300s on European routes, which had served as feeders between Stockholm and Oslo, to and from the Copenhagen hub. Instead we established several direct routes from Stockholm and Oslo to numerous cities, using the smaller DC9s. We also established a clearer distinction between business class and tourist class. Business passengers received many valuable benefits: faster check-in using special counters, higher luggage weight allowances, their own special priority tags for check-in luggage, opportunity to be last on board and first off upon landing, greater seat space making it possible to work with a little privacy, superior service with better food, drinks and newspapers, and personal information about arrival times and connections to other flights.

At Kastrup, a separate business lounge was built offering light refreshments, business facilities, and telephone and telex services (this was before cell phones!). Business passengers could get help with booking and rebooking of tickets, and personal information about departure times and possible changes.

Nevertheless, the biggest challenge was internal. SAS was a top-heavy organization where middle management made virtually all decisions concerning individual passengers or freight shipments. Employees closest to customers had few opportunities to influence customer experience. Even simple operations, such as rebooking and ticket upgrades, had to be handled by middle management. Therefore, those who really knew what customers wanted were completely hampered in doing so. It was as if the forward on a soccer team had to ask the coach on the sidelines if he could score, instead of taking advantage of his chances for a goal. Everyone did as well as possible, but the responsibility was misplaced. People were used to being told what to do instead of finding solutions themselves.

A survey showed that every single passenger, on average, was in contact with SAS employees four times over the course of a journey. The average duration of the contact was 15 seconds. In essence, that was the customers' opportunity to determine whether they were treated well or poorly, and whether they would travel with SAS again or recommend the company to others. Today, those encounters are probably even fewer since many features are Web-based.

From these simple facts, it was easy to see that we had to flatten the organization and add a lot more responsibility at the operational level. Hence the motto "Tear down the pyramids!" which was also the Scandinavian title of the book Carlzon wrote later.

The first step in the process was to create a mutual understanding of the situation among all managers and employees. This was no small task for a business with 20,000 employees. The numbers were clear: the company steadily plunged toward a deficit—for the second year in a row. Despite this, there were many who regarded the decline as temporary. Another viewpoint quite typical for heavily top-controlled businesses is that the responsibility for finding solutions to problems always rests higher up— or at least somewhere else in the organization.

Every opportunity was used to create the most common picture of the new market situation and how inadequate the company was organized in relation to it. SAS management, thereby, hoped that most would see that there was a great need for change and would help to find solutions.

One of the measures taken to help employees understand the change process was the publication of a little red book, which was handed out to everyone. It was called *Nu skal vi börja slåss* (*Let's Get In There and Fight!*). Internally it was nicknamed *Janne's Little Red* after Chinese Chairman Mao Tse-Tung's little red book, which described in quotation form the theory and methods of the Cultural Revolution and other brutal change processes that transformed China from a poor emperor dictatorship to a modern Communist, Marxist-Leninist and ostensible utopia. *Mao's Little Red* became widespread by the end of the 1960s in the leftist environments in the West. It became the Marxist-Leninists' bible around the world, including the Palestinian and German terrorist movements that swept through Europe when I was studying in Nuremberg. For many of them, the little book was the rationale and recipe for armed revolution.

Carlzon's recipe for an effective turnaround was, of course, far from Mao's. But perhaps the little book still produced some of the same effect that such writings can give in certain situations where the Bible gives the Christian power and the Koran gives the Muslim strength.

In any case, the effect far exceeded expectations. *Janne's Little Red* was of crucial importance in the SAS change process. The hope was that everyone would understand that the measures selected were necessary—whether or not the individual departments or functions liked them.

The initial "gospel" was signed by Carlzon personally. It was short and clear:

> We have to fight in a stagnant market. We must fight against competitors who are more efficient than we are and that are at least as

good as we are in promoting the best deals. We can do it, but only if we are prepared to fight. Side by side. We are all in this together.

Then a simple narrative began accompanied by line drawings, as in a children's book. Aircraft and other relevant shapes were humanized with mouth and eyes that reinforced the content and mood of the text. And, as with children's books, there were only a few lines on each page. The language was almost free of foreign words and typical organizational / financial terms that business managers often resort to when attempting to explain the necessity for making changes in a company. In return—or for that reason—the descriptions were crystal clear and citable, just as with Mao, Jesus, and Muhammad.

Under the drawing of a smiling airplane was the text:

We were a healthy and profitable company for 17 years. Business prospered year after year. We sat in IATA (International Air Transport Association) with other airlines and pretty much agreed on how we were going to share a steadily growing goody bag. It was a safe and orderly world.

Who knew there were storm clouds over the horizon?

The untroubled plane cannot know this when it flies from one side of the globe toward dark clouds waiting on the other side.

Suddenly, the storm breaks loose . . .

We see the poor, innocent plane assaulted by lightning and thunder from pitch-black clouds with the words:

New and independent airlines! – Sharpened competition over the Atlantic! – Increased fuel prices! – Increasing costs! – Higher prices! – Reduced demand! – Price war! – Deficit!

So it continued with banal, almost infantile illustrations, but the short lyrics were effective. Whether you were the director or operations assistant, it was impossible not to relate to his simple but accurate descriptions of the situation:

The airline lost 12 million US dollars last year. We are going to lose money this year, as well. But it must stop. We cannot afford to lose any more.

We are in a bad state of affairs, but we have not reached the critical point yet. If we had, we wouldn't have known how to get our nose back up.

But we can do it. If we are ready to fight for our jobs and our future, we can get back in good health.

It will not be easy. We carry a pile of unnecessary costs from those comfortable days under IATA's umbrella of protection. Now we need to trim away the fat.

Followed by some telling examples:

In the United States, Delta Airlines serves and freights 120% more passengers per employee than SAS. The American company will additionally score 14% to 40% higher than SAS in the most central profitability indicators.

Among the old competitors in Europe, Swissair managed to adapt to the new competitive conditions. The Swiss airline still earns money and generates higher margins than SAS in all areas, which means that Swissair's operating results are heading up toward the 3.5% plus mark, while SAS is heading down toward the 0.3% minus mark. Unless we do something, this gap will increase.

The first economic objective was to turn a loss of 12 million US dollars to a surplus of the same amount. That required only 2 percent increased efficiency in all work processes: a modest goal. But at the same time, Carlzon warned that in a few years another zero had to be added, so that the result had to be at least 120 million US dollars. He just as clearly worded the alternative to this development: "Our condition is going to be disastrous if we don't manage it."

This, of course, makes a convincing impression. In less robust organizations, it could perhaps have intimidated people into insecurity and poor self-esteem, with similar results. But at that time at SAS, it was appropriate to maintain a little threat behind the request. Most organizations, which had begun to fade because they sat too long on their laurels, needed a mix of carrot and whip—and hope.

Thus, *Janne's Little Red* contained the recipe for what needed to be done, along with a healthy dose of optimism:

We need to be more efficient. We need to consolidate. We need
to become more market oriented. After my first few months in
the company, I am convinced: We have the will to work. We want
to take responsibility. We have the knowledge. Our new goal
and result-oriented organization will turn all these powers loose.

The entire company was evaluated across business
areas, departments, and management layers. All features
that seemed unlikely to contribute to making SAS the best
company for frequent-flyer traveling businessmen were
discontinued or reorganized. Necessary functions were
strengthened. This resulted in 147 small and large projects, which entailed an additional investment of 260 million Norwegian crowns and annual additional costs of 60
million Norwegian crowns. However, we no longer called
these *expenses* but *resources*. After one more critical evaluation of resources, spending decreased in other areas by
200 million US dollars.

The company would still operate according to its
three main objectives—*safety, punctuality,* and *service*—but
now these were powerfully revitalized. Safety was still
paramount and had to be the basis for all evaluations and
decisions. Punctuality received higher priority; for example, aircraft that previously waited for late deliveries from
SAS catering simply took off after consulting with passengers who felt it was more important to be on schedule than
to eat and drink on board. Instead, they received a form of
compensation. This did not happen many times. The catering company discovered quickly that it profited more

by fine-tuning delivery routines than by not being paid for their goods. The solution was accountability in the form of freedom to find the best solutions; in experiencing that, there were consequences when one did not deliver in line with goals and expectations.

The company's *space control* in Copenhagen responsible for the company's capacity management received the additional task of monitoring and reporting punctuality. The report was posted directly to a separate screen in Carlzon's Stockholm office. This move was duly communicated throughout the organization and made such a strong impression that some questioned whether punctuality was more important than safety. Thus, of course, it was conveyed that the top boss got all reports of discrepancies in relation to safety via the same system.

The truth was that, indeed, the screen was in Carlzon's office, but it was never connected. If it had been connected, it would hardly have been of much use because the CEO rarely sat in the office. Most of the time he was in meetings or on the road. In that sense, one could very well say that his personal commitment continually posed a risk of discovery for lack of punctuality, but not in the form of monitoring.

All employees who had contact with customers took courses in service. Meanwhile they received extended powers to make necessary decisions to please the customers. Instead of someone sitting in an office and deciding what to serve the passengers on board various routes, the cabin crew was invited to define the needs and make suggestions as to what was possible to serve. The result was an improvement in both the product variety and service—without significantly higher costs. Similarly, all other groups of employees were encouraged to redefine and widen their assignments based on what they experienced customers wanted and what was the most efficient way to do the job.

It had a profound effect: both customers' and employees' feelings of well-being rose—not to mention efficiency and pride. Soon the process led to positive business results. After only one year, SAS posted a profit, which continued for several years to come. Then the process began to lose some of its power, as always happens when good systems and effective follow-up procedures are not established.

The reason was banal: in our eagerness to make the visible customer portion responsible, similar measures were not implemented to prepare middle management for what the turnaround would require of them. That was a huge mistake, which made it difficult to meet new challenges while maintaining life in the ongoing process. Unfortunately, this mistake was identified too late, requiring considerable extra work later.

As a member of the project team and centrally placed in management of the intercontinental routes, I was in a position to get the maximum out of the first part of the turnaround. Leading something in development always gives one more power and credit than liquidating departments. I was definitely on the "yes team" during the change process. Where I would have ended up had I led a department that was to be downsized is hard to say. It has to be unpleasant to to find that what one has been doing for years is suddenly worth nothing. On the other hand, I never doubted that SAS had to implement several essential tactics to become more competitive before I joined the project team.

Based on the results we achieved with the international routes, it became clear to me that I would continue to work very closely with top management at the head office in Stockholm. One day, the boss of SAS Norway called me in. He wanted to discuss something regarding the cargo department. I thought he would offer some views on how to implement the freight department in the new strategy, since I was close to the process and had worked with cargo in the past. The agenda for the meeting, however, was much more concrete: the company needed a new boss for SAS Cargo Norway. The position would involve my joining the central management group for SAS Cargo and the management group for SAS Norway.

My immediate reaction was that this was a little odd because I had been in the forefront of the new strategy work on the passenger side with the development of the intercontinental routes. Now I would somehow revert to my student days and the subject of my thesis at Nuremberg. Perhaps I was also becoming somewhat affected by the old cultural attitude that influenced SAS during the time I was there: It was more honorable to work with passengers and, in particular, the concept of The Businessman's Airline, which was the most important driver of long-haul trips. This represented the most visible and proudest part of the company. Freight was something one did on the side: since the plane was already taking off with passengers, one might as well fill it with goods, too.

But after I found out what the job entailed, I became excited. A project for developing a strategy for cargo had been initiated but not yet completed, and they wanted me in on some of it. The market for air cargo transport was growing rapidly, not just in Norway where the aquaculture industry was about to develop into an export industry. Only aircraft could bring fresh salmon quickly enough to markets in the Far East and the United States. SAS was the natural airline and could probably gain a leading position in this market if the company adapted to customer needs.

In 1982, SAS Cargo Norway yielded poor results. There were significant internal conflicts; the turnaround underway in the rest of the company had clearly not penetrated here. When I found out that I would have a free hand to develop business both internally and externally, I felt the same excitement as when I started to get the hang of the job at Lufthansa catering. There were so many opportunities and challenges here that I might possibly achieve something. Another positive side: the whole family could move home to Norway from the United States.

After I took over the new position in Norway, the turnaround at SAS reached its first climax. In the middle of April 1983, it was time for a formidable kick-off of the "new

SAS." It started in the main hangar at Fornebu in Oslo on April 13, continued in Copenhagen later that day and in Stockholm the following day. The ceremony in Copenhagen is described in the book *Förnyelsens ledarskap—Från flygbolag til reseföretag* (*Renewal Leadership—From Airlines to Travel Companies*), written by three Swedish researchers who followed developments at SAS in the 1980s:

> VD Janne Carlzon held a short speech: 'We have brought SAS back to good service and profitability – better service has made for better profitability,' he said. 'SAS has turned toward the market and is now showing a new face. We are achieving a facelift that mirrors key internal changes. Every detail in our change process shall support our strategy for The Businessman's Airline.'

Then the authors describe the ceremony's most magical moment when the hangar ports suddenly opened and in rolled a newly lacquered, white DC9 with stripes in the Scandinavian flag colors of red, white, blue, and yellow under the belly.

> A murmur went through the audience. The plane stopped. The doors opened and out came the pilots, flight attendants and ground personnel, one by one, presented by two masters of ceremonies, a man and a woman. It was like a fashion show, but with employees on stage instead of models.

Calvin Klein had designed each outfit in collaboration with a consultant and working groups of employees who had provided input on how the new uniforms would be both "convenient and attractive," another example of how the employees had been involved in the turnaround.

In the cargo department, we were content with everyday clothes and embarked in a process that was considered less glamorous but no less challenging.

Angelika was happy to move to Norway for the first time. We had good friends here from our student years in Nuremberg. We had my parents and family, and old friends that Angelika also knew. It was important that the boys were closer to their Norwegian grandparents whom they had hardly seen while living in the United States and Sweden. We no longer had financial problems. I received benefits for leading SAS Cargo Norway that enabled Angelika to stay home with the boys. We all experienced it as positive—perhaps even necessary.

But even though we purchased a great piece of land and built a house in Høvik with a view toward Fornebu, there was one drawback: I was rarely home.

7
CARGO'S SALARY

The challenges at SAS Cargo Norway were greater than I had imagined. Many of the same attitudes characterized the culture that we had experienced on the passenger side of business: customers adapted the shipping service SAS found easiest and most convenient for SAS to deliver. In effect, the organization was divided between two managers who both reported directly to the SAS Cargo manager in Stockholm. One was responsible for logistics—cargo freight terminals and cargo merchandise handling; the other was responsible for sales and marketing.

The new signals that had come from top management calling for a flatter structure and more customer-oriented operations had split the managers in their opinions on how best to run the Norwegian cargo shipping department. The sales and marketing manager tried to bring in sales and customized services tailored to customers' needs. Backed by support from his own and higher ranks, the operations manager insisted that it was difficult to supply additional services beyond what they had already organized.

In reality, it was a power struggle between the two managers, which naturally filtered down through the organization causing endless conflicts. For several years, SAS reinforced this by filling SAS Cargo with people who, for various reasons, had not fit in any departments on the passenger side of the business and who worked in shipping against their will. Without coordination at the management level, the two managers had no control over customer promises or deliveries, even though they were both diligent workers.

Uncertainty and, thus, the need for control comes with lack of leadership. There was a strong focus regimen in the operations department, which ensured that all deliveries were correct according to the current procedures and rules. "It won't work" was the standard reply to any and all proposals made by the sales and marketing department. The reasons given were always technical, logistical, or monetary in nature.

The results followed. Profits were down. The company lost money on many agreements with major customers. In return, many small cargo customers paid exorbitant prices. I almost felt that the rationale "the planes still go" prevailed in some parts of the organization when it came to pricing services. In practice, it meant that both small cargo customers and passengers paid for the major customers' freight. In other words, there was no consistent thought behind the value given by customers to shipping services, probably because no one had established a basis for what value the services actually provided to customers.

I also discovered that the only thing that had been measured was the effort in terms of production and productivity—not the results. This is like when police measure how many hours they patrol the streets but don't make the connection to reduced crime; or keep track of time getting to crime scenes but not whether they get there in time to defuse a demanding situation or to save human lives. Not to mention measuring a teacher only by how many hours he or she teaches and not by what kind of marks and development his or her students achieve—as is the case in Norwegian schools. The national tests do not actually measure the individual teacher.

Organizations that do not measure the results of their efforts become very static. They miss milestones and, consequently, have little to show for it. At the same time, there is generally a low level of awareness as to whether actions produce good or bad results, which makes it very difficult to initiate effective turnarounds. Why should you change yourself or the systems when you pretty much meet the production targets set out in the business plans?

Only when you set clear and measurable goals for the expected results—and dare to compare them with similar businesses—can you form a complete picture of whether you are doing well or poorly. Then starting processes become meaningful when everyone can find out how to improve. I realized that SAS Cargo Norway really needed this kind of organizational development.

With my promotion in February 1982, the department received one manager. It was a good foundation but only a baby step toward a more cohesive organization, where 400 people had partly been directed by two different regimes and partly operated at their sole discretion. Leaders who believe that they can change an organization solely by virtue of their own strengths have likely developed a self-image and assertiveness that makes them unfit to lead turnarounds. If there is anything a leader needs when he or she comes from outside and into a mismanaged organization, it is humility and patience.

First, I found out if either of the two managers would remain with the company. It turned out that the operations manager was on his way out, while Sales and Marketing Manager Egil Budde assumed that he would be the new manager. That didn't happen. Nevertheless, instead of competing with me as the department's leader, he gave me a genuine and warm welcome. He was a very loyal and indispensable employee, and realized right away that the new market orientation in SAS would now also apply to the cargo business. That was what he had been fighting for—without success.

Budde turned out to be a great salesman. He now had the time and space to develop his best qualities. It was as though he was created to get the new customer orientation operating by helping customers feel that the company now adapted SAS services to their needs.

SAS Cargo Norway had cargo terminals in Oslo, Bergen, Stavanger, Trondheim, Bodø, and Tromsø. Each had its own freight manager. The largest terminals had their own sales representative. In addition, SAS accepted cargo from all the other airports. The station's ground personnel handled cargo operations. On paper, there was a distinct organization, but in practice, both culture and logistics were ill-suited for the market.

After visiting all the terminals around the country and having some beneficial meetings with trade unions, I quickly realized that if we were to push through the needed changes, we had to create a completely new business culture. We had to do the same as we did on the passenger side of the business: move the responsibility and tasks out to those who actually worked with customers. At the same time, we needed to get all middle managers on the team; it wasn't just individual attitudes toward customers that needed change, but also systems and logistics. This involved organizational measures, which again required leadership.

We also saw that the sales side of the business was incorrectly localized and sized relative to market and customer needs. This was particularly true with regard to the new aquaculture industry. This currently strong-growth industry was dependent on quick transportation of its products. Customers had largely come to SAS of their own initiative. With more effort on the sales side, and better utilization and adaptation of our cargo freight capacity, we would probably be able to significantly increase volumes.

We put a number of processes in place to enable the entire organization to meet the new demands and opportunities in the market. At that time, many Norwegian companies experimented with *quality circles*, a Japanese method that made employee groups responsible for developing and managing *best practices* in their daily routine. This provided limited results. The method was based on a collective mind-set, which, as prosperity increased, was fading in the Norwegian workforce at the time. Quality circles also demanded an enormous amount of follow-up and coordination in a business with almost 400 employees.

We ultimately chose to engage a consultant whom I already knew, Roald Nomme. He ran the consulting firm Scandinavian Management Consultants, which SAS owned and had already used in the turnaround on the passenger side of the business. First, we ran a couple of thorough situation analyses, but they kept coming out lopsided because many employees would not participate for fear of being identified and held responsible for their possibly critical remarks.

This is a known phenomenon in organizations with weak management and strong control. Uncertainty and insecurity typify the climate. Disagreement is interpreted as disloyalty and distrust; suggestions for change are perceived as a threat. Making changes in such organizations first requires restoring confidence and reassurance. The first step is to accept that the situation is as it is and then start the process from there.

When all were promised that only external consultants would handle the answers and that, in addition, people could remain anonymous, all took part in the survey. It showed much the same as I had seen in other SAS departments: both employees and middle managers had little understanding of the overall picture of which they were a part. They felt greater responsibility for following ingrained routines and rules than they did in creating satisfied customers. The fear of failing followed.

Due to the results of the survey, we sent all middle managers to courses in coaching, a management style that deals with helping the individual employee take initiative in the choice of solutions. I followed up all the processes personally and was present at the beginning of all the courses to supply the necessary authority to both the courses and course leaders. At the same time, I used the opportunity to draw up the slightly larger lines so that everyone understood the context in which he or she was now supposed to be a leader and what goals we were trying to achieve.

It was incredibly pleasurable to watch the process begin to work. On the home front, though, we met few of the expectations. What we had thought and hoped would be a kind of "eight to four at the office" existence meant more traveling than ever before—and considerably more stress. For now, there were no long flight distances where I could work, relax, or sleep, but tight schedules and short journeys throughout Norway. I was frequently at management meetings at SAS Cargo in Stockholm, which were often lengthy due to the turnaround in the entire airline company. I also spent a lot of time in Copenhagen, the cargo hub for air freight through the SAS Cargo Center where I sat on the board.

Budde was the one who got sales and marketing moving in Norway. He really understood what SAS actually sold. What mattered was not shipping of fish but helping customers sell the fish in the United States and other countries at the best possible price. In the beginning, he even took fresh salmon with him when he traveled to New York. He always had advance reservations at the most prominent restaurants in the Big Apple, where upon arrival, he asked permission to deliver the fish personally to the kitchen so the chefs could test it.

The reception was overwhelming. The salmon, which was pulled out of the sea off Norway either that same day or late the day before (when one took the time difference into account) was fresher than what they got from their own or Canadian waters. The next time, he ordered a table at another restaurant and got the same reaction. It wasn't a difficult choice for restaurants that survive off serving the best of the best: they had to buy salmon from Norway.

In this manner, Budde identified so strongly with the mission that eventually he—and not a salmon exporter—got the nickname Mr. Salmon from a rapidly growing number of importers in the United States. A transportation services provider could hardly get a better testimonial. He knew, of course, that the more the salmon exporters sold "over there," the greater the revenue for SAS.

We continually tried to think out of the box. In collaboration with salmon exporters and packaging manufacturers, we eventually developed better packaging that could hold the right temperature and humidity. In the absence of advanced measuring equipment, we even had people go into the cargo hold on a regular basis along the way and take measurements inside the cartons to ensure the fish held stable conditions across the Atlantic. This was done to develop the optimal packaging with the optimal amount of ice to secure the right temperature and moisture.

This was a straightforward operation on a Boeing 747 Combi since the passenger cabin was on the same deck. This flight was perfect for both freight and passengers because it was so flexible. It could be rigged with 205 to 270 seats in front and could take between 6 and 12 load containers in the rear. If it had been necessary to transport live fish over the Atlantic Ocean, I'm sure that Budde and company could have done that too.

Budde and I complemented each other in a phenomenal way. I could never have achieved the same results with customers that he did. At the same time, I think it would have been demanding for him to carry out all the organizational changes that had to happen logistically and still sell as much as he did. I dare say that we brought out the best in each other, and that our way of working together rubbed off on the rest of the organization. There is nothing more contagious in an organization than leader behavior—whether good or bad.

Unfortunately, many managers are far too concerned with personal positions and end up in jobs for which they are not suited. Those ill-suited to their responsibilities and tasks rarely act with enough confidence to inspire coworkers to be as good as or better than themselves. They often view the best people as competitors and either take credit for their performance or prevent them from performing up to par. There is little room for disagreement with these managers. They consider a proposal that goes against their own ideas as a threat—until they realize it might be a good idea—then they steal it and announce it a little later as their own without crediting the originator. There is little to motivate employees in such circumstances.

The battle for positions negatively affects efficiency. When people think more about what they can do for their own position than about what is best for the company, they actually undermine themselves. Nevertheless, we often see managers moved up in the hierarchy who are primarily concerned with positioning themselves. Like politicians, they use every opportunity to state what they have accomplished; and they always have something coming down the pike. Thus, their proficiency and worth are exaggerated.

People who only work for themselves, and not for the business, easily move upward in businesses with closed cultures and low awareness of what produces good results. Things going sour and poor results are inevitable. The higher up the ladder they are, the greater the consequences for the business.

We saw fast results from the process; there was tremendous growth in the aquaculture industry. There seemed to be an insatiable market for fresh salmon in Japan and the United States. With better-adapted shipping routes, more participants could increase exports. In the beginning, the cargo terminal at Gardermoen in Oslo shipped less than 20 tons of salmon per day. In the course of one year, this increased to 52 tons to the United States and 20 tons to Tokyo per day.

But a new problem arose: we no longer made money on this cargo. We had agreed to special terms to get the export of salmon started. With the new volumes, salmon shipping took capacity away from other cargo where we had normal rates. On some routes, it took up all capacity. Shipping salmon had become so extensive that we no longer considered it as marginal goods. Instead, it became a problem of re-dimensioning our capacity. We could not live with that. In the long term, salmon exporters could not live with it either, for that would mean we would not be able to give their products top priority. Thus, the fish would arrive in degraded condition.

Thanks to the close relationship we had developed with these customers, we were able to bring them on board the process for setting a new pricing structure. After calculating a reasonable income distribution for the increased exports, for which SAS Cargo Norway had a significant part of the credit and which had evolved from a random transport service to a tailored one, we were able to increase prices by 300 percent. In particular, our changes in capacity, quality, and availability allowed customers to make more money because they sold fresher merchandise for a higher price. Salmon exporters initially had very high margins. Customers were, therefore, willing to pay more for the shipping.

I think this is a good example of how one can develop a good working relationship between customer and supplier by putting one's cards on the table. Mutual benefit and transparency creates commitment for both parties.

No one is tempted to squeeze the other or go behind the other's back. Dependable and sustainable business is to let everyone get a rightful share of the profits.

Suddenly air cargo became an important business area for SAS. In some areas, we did as much business as the most profitable passenger routes. We represented The Businessman's Airline as well as anyone; we had not only exporters on board, but also their products. The only difference was that the products had a one-way ticket, while exporters had to buy round-trip tickets to come home again.

I still regard the turnaround at SAS Cargo Norway as one of the most important lessons I went through after my oral exam in Nuremberg and my hopeless first few weeks as a ticket salesman in Chicago. I had managed to get through both of them alone, perhaps thanks to my childhood experiences when Dad sent me around the world and, at times, I felt lost. Now I was successful as a leader and discovered that leadership is really all about one thing: do what you can to do good to others no matter where your starting point is.

After two years, I had just started to implement an improvement process for SAS Cargo Norway when I was summoned to a meeting at the Stockholm headquarters with top management. I was constantly in meetings with other departments and assumed that they also wanted to discuss something about air cargo since we flew so much salmon on the long haul routes.

Their agenda, however, was just as different from my assumptions as they had been when I was summoned into the Norwegian CEO's office two years before. Now they wanted me to be the head of SAS in the United States. There were challenges there at least as great as in the cargo department in Norway. Some areas were in critical condition, both in terms of cargo and passengers. A turnaround had to be implemented by someone who knew both the SAS system and the United States. Carlzon, the group CEO, personally sponsored my candidacy.

I was still a young man, barely 38 years old. What could I do? Say no? If I did, most likely the doors to other exciting tasks in the airline would slowly close. What would I say to Angelika and the boys? Should I tear the family up by the roots yet again? Admittedly, they had enjoyed the United States the last time. Now, though, Norway was important: even though I was traveling a lot, there was still some semblance of a family life.

I was both happy and fearful when I sat on the plane back to Oslo. Happy because there was extensive recognition in the new job offer and because I knew that Angelika also would be happy for me—but what would she say to moving again?

8

"YOU MAKE THE DIFFERENCE"

SAS in North America, with its 600 employees, had offices spread all over the continent, from Los Angeles in the West to Boston in the East, Miami in the South, and Montreal in the North. The head office was located close to John F. Kennedy International Airport (JFK) in New York. We had several daily departures to Scandinavia from New York, Chicago, Los Angeles, and Seattle. SAS also had its largest cargo terminal at JFK.

The head of SAS in North America reported to the head of the intercontinental routes in Stockholm. I took over the job from a pleasant Norwegian whose assistant I had been when I worked in New York after my stay in Chicago. He had managed SAS for many years in the United States and had been involved with changing large parts of the route pattern for long-distance flights. But he had not initiated any of the internal organizational changes that the ongoing turnaround required. That was the reason for my takeover. In reality, it was a generational change.

I discovered immediately that the organization was heavily top managed and that those top people worked poorly together. All operational decisions came from the top and filtered down through the ranks. On the way down, these messages were diluted, twisted, and fragmented so that, in practice, the further people were from the top the more they acted according to their own preference. To remedy that, we initiated a variety of control measures, which, unfortunately, did not work. Instead, suspicions arose and productivity declined.

It was obvious that many employees did not have the opportunity to take advantage of their potential for productive work. Instead, much energy was lost in what I felt were unnecessary conflicts. Commitment and openness were secondary. The worst problems were at the cargo terminal in New York, resulting in damage, thefts, discrepancies, and significant delays. With no real responsibility on the part of those who handled the cargo, no one did anything about the deviations other than to report them. Thus, a lack of culture ruled.

The Teamsters union, known to be powerful and contentious, was right in the middle of the problems at the JFK cargo terminal. Except for making demands, the union had little or no communication with SAS management. It seemed that management had pulled away from the union's representatives rather than try to solve the problems together. I remember I was warned not to get too close to them because the Mafia was said to control the Teamsters.

Since I was familiar with a large part of the SAS US organization, I was given a quick overview of the challenges. Nevertheless, I visited all the offices to get my own current picture of the situation. It was beneficial, for it turned out that there was a lot to play with. All our station managers and a lot of our office managers were operationally skilled. They were very important for the development of the company going forward.

During this tour, I, of course, took the opportunity to say a little about the ongoing turnaround of SAS and in turn obtained insights on how to carry it out in North America. There was little openness in the beginning, as there always is in organizations that have been heavily controlled from the top. Still, I think the tour was a good idea. The earlier employees are involved in a change process, giving them the feeling they may have some influence, the more smoothly the process will continue. Ownership results in motivation and less resistance.

As expected, the biggest problems were at the main office in New York—at the top of the organization all the way out to the job location, and especially at the cargo terminal. There was also an enormous distance between the top and bottom. The previous management team had barely shown themselves on the floor.

I remember how surprised many of the employees were the first time I climbed up on a stack of pallets in the midst of the cargo terminal to introduce myself as their new boss. Most of them looked at me strangely. It was obvious that they were not used to visits from upper-level managers, especially not rubbing elbows with them between containers, cargo, and forklifts. Some were surely skeptical, but there was no hostile atmosphere. I remember seeing more expectation in their puzzled faces than seeing fear.

There was an arrangement for supervisors at the cargo terminal, who were sort of bosses in my opinion but without the formal powers that real foremen would have had. They had higher wages than the others but were still ordinary members of the union. On paper, they should have contributed to organizing and leading the work, but they couldn't implement any changes or sanctions when the work did not go according to plan. That responsibility rested on a higher level. I quickly realized that I had to establish a good relationship with these supervisors. It turned out that their job positions were created primarily as a pay driver so the union could have some differences to play with in wage negotiations.

I had learned how important it was to be on good terms with the unions at SAS Cargo Norway. Without getting the employees' unions on the team, it is almost impossible to carry out turnarounds that produce lasting results. There was only one trade union to deal with at SAS United States, but it was the fearsome Teamsters union, which ruled the cargo terminal and the JFK station. I defied all warnings and invited the leaders to a meeting. I felt nothing worse could happen than that they would just reject the request.

When a black Cadillac rolled up in front of the office at the cargo terminal where we were to meet and three men in black leather coats, gloves, and hats rose out of that big rig, I admit that, briefly, I had second thoughts. Yet, the three professional and pleasant gentlemen behind the somewhat intense exterior began by saying that they appreciated that

I had invited them to a meeting. That was a rarity, and they basically felt that it was high time a new boss had taken over.

I had no other objectives at that first meeting than to introduce myself and learn their views on SAS and our business in the United States. They were honest and said they knew there were problems at the cargo terminal. I stated that I was worried about the situation; all the losses and sloppiness undermined the company's morale and profitability, and thus everyone's opportunities to earn an honest day's wage. I stressed that the majority of those who worked there were honest and respectable people. The problem was weak leadership at the cargo terminal. Since the supervisors had no formal authority either, it was difficult to sort out the few rotten apples that ruined it for everyone. What would the Teamsters union say if the supervisors received status as genuine middle managers with management responsibility and training?

The three union leaders thought that was just great. They believed it could help resolve the situation, which they also considered worrisome. On the lowest middle manager level, there was no reason they couldn't continue as union members. Rather the contrary. The Teamsters union wanted to organize people with management responsibilities, as long as the other members in the workplace accepted it. They felt that it would go smoothly.

We parted with a friendly handshake and a shared desire for continued cooperation. A short time later, workers who had taken advantage of the leeway that weak leadership had given them were out of the cargo terminal—

without anyone in leadership having to lift a finger. I don't know how it happened: they were just gone. Thefts and damage disappeared with them, and cargo handling suddenly went smoothly. Later it came out, probably due to the cleanup, that one of the formal leaders of the cargo terminal had helped himself to the employees' welfare fund. He was weeded out quickly.

I then invited managers from various levels to a meeting to hammer out a strategy for the US business that was in line with the new guidelines from the parent company. It was the first time the leadership in New York had invited them in on a real process. It turned out—as it usually did—that those who led the operational units had a lot of good input: ideas about what we should aim for in the United States and how we should organize the work and ourselves in order to accomplish it.

Meanwhile, I discovered that there was a certain gap in management experience and in the manner that the departments were run. I suggested, therefore, that we all go through a leadership development program tailored for us by the Center for Creative Leadership (CCL). It was already one of the most prestigious leadership development institutions in the United States at the time and is still among the world's foremost institutions in its field. For me, it would be the introduction to a long-lasting partnership, which would end up with my being chairman of the board of the institution today.

At that time, the leadership role was viewed differently in the United States as well as elsewhere in the world.

Some of the same attitudes that my old boss at Lufthansa had conveyed in his book *We Up Here, You Down There* still existed. When my contacts at CCL heard that I had supervisors who were members of the Teamsters among the participants, and that I would include them in management training, they wondered if I had lost my judgment. They thought it would ruin everything and undermine management's credibility. The trade union members would be able to use this in pitting employees against management when it came to wage negotiation, working environment issues, and other situations that could end in labor disputes.

I said that I was convinced they would be loyal, precisely because of the fact that we included them in the management group. Through the strategy work and leadership development program, they would have the opportunity to influence the turnaround, as well as have the same picture of the goals, challenges, and solutions as the rest of the company's management team. And, I continued, they would become important ambassadors rather than conspirators.

Some might have said they could be perceived as hostages. That was never a subject of discussion. I continued to have regular talks with the three Teamsters leaders. Their feedback was that they thought the new middle management system at the cargo terminal worked perfectly. Through these meetings, I got an ever better impression of the union's work. Of course, it had to safeguard members' interests as its overall goal. That occurred based on two main strategies. When they dealt with business leaders who cooperated and included them, they contributed with all their power and resources to help the business do well. Against leaders who perceived them as enemies, they were ruthless opponents. I saw nothing of the alleged Mafia methods, beyond pressure they apparently had used and group dynamics to remove dishonest elements.

The leadership development program consisted of three one-week-long sessions. I was present at all the sessions and participated on an equal footing with everyone else. Some top managers refuse to participate in leadership development programs, either because they have an overexaggerated opinion of their capabilities and believe only middle managers need to develop themselves, or because they are afraid to show weakness. That reduces the effect of the program as an engine for developing the entire business. Lack of participation by top managers signals to those below that development is not necessary for everyone, and if you consider yourself a full-fledged leader you can evade common processes.

A manager's strongest management tool is always his own conduct. No speeches or documents, though richly laden with desired conditions and pious thoughts about the future, can make up for what the manager actually does—and does *not*—do: not words but actions. That is how others perceive corporate law. That does not mean that the manager has to come up with everything. Rather the contrary. Many of the best ideas come jointly due to good work processes. But the manager must be the foremost in living up to them if he or she is going to get others onto the team.

I saw how the leadership development program contributed toward welding us together into a single team. We honored each other and ourselves. A team is not sufficiently sustainable—and effective—unless all players on the team know each other's strengths and weaknesses. Only then will they know how to bring the best out of one another and what it takes so everyone can help to improve.

We all went through the Myers-Briggs personality test, a very thorough analysis that aims primarily to increase awareness of the type of person you are as a human being based on a set of criteria. In which directions do you most lean:

- Introverted or extroverted?
- Thinking or feeling?
- Intuitive or sensing?
- Judging or perceiving?

There is no right or wrong result of this analysis. It only points out the kind of aspects you need to develop further. You have to know yourself and your own development potential in order to be able to lead and develop others. Whether you are a leader at the top or intermediate level, it is important to receive feedback about yourself. Then you are aware of what you need in order to continue development. It is also the best medicine against becoming so great in your own eyes that you lose ground contact—a phenomenon that particularly affects top executives, and one that I have found myself close to at times.

Intensive leadership development leads to some dropouts. Not all feel secure enough to confront themselves through others' feedback. In our process, no one dropped out. The most likely reason was that the program was so tailored to the SAS situation and to the main strategy, which all felt they had helped formulate. In addition, after a relatively short period, we felt we got an answer when the market response showed that we were on the right path, and the results began to point in the right direction. That made it easier to gain acceptance of the overall strategy.

One of the principle measures in our strategy was to shift attention from sales volume to results. Instead of filling up planes with the most passengers, we would now propel marketing and sales based on earnings per passenger. This was much of the thinking behind The Businessman's Airline, both on the passenger and cargo side. Even a half-full plane with full-paying passengers is better business than a full tourist plane. Of course, we wanted to try to fill up planes as much as possible, but now tourist class passengers and discounted cargo would come as additional income to an aircraft that was already profitable with full-paying passengers or freight at mainstream prices.

For the next step in the process, all managers would run local strategy processes for their respective stations/ offices and departments involving all coworkers in the new plans for the company. They ran according to the same principle as the leader development program: every employee would have the greatest possible freedom and responsibility to find the best solutions for implementing the strategy. It worked very well and resulted in a number of contributions. These were collected and presented at a kick-off meeting for strategy and clarification of expectations under the motto "You Make the Difference." It was going to be one of the big events of which I was a part during my time with SAS.

Afterward, while all the station managers and station employees were at a seminar, the headquarters personnel would support their functions. Once, it was my turn to substitute as station manager in New York. It ended with a very embarrassing episode that was instructive, but one that I could well have done without.

SAS had three departures to Scandinavia scheduled to take off at about the same time. A technical error popped up on one departure just as we were going to board the passengers. We had no idea how long it would take to fix. So we started to move passengers from one flight to another. In the meantime, they found the problem. Then we chose to move the passengers back again, inflicting significant delays on all departures.

While my secretary worked feverishly on this, I tried, without success, to hold the passengers' attention by talking. In the first place, they asked a number of questions I could not answer. In the second, I was not used to standing in front of a swarm of stressed and angry customers.

But the worst part was that I was afraid I would be recognized. What would the passengers think about SAS when not even one of their top bosses had oversight of the chaos? I was also probably the most stressed of all. I'm sure the passengers noticed it, even though I tried to be amiable.

This was an excellent but hard lesson. An experienced coworker working at the check-in would probably have made completely different decisions than I did, keeping his or her cool in the face of the disgruntled passengers. The episode was one more affirmation of the philosophy behind the turnaround in the entire SAS and the leader development programs. The ones who meet the customers are the ones sitting closest to the solutions. So it must be in daily operation. As leaders, we must assume that they have it under control and know which direction the wind blows at all times.

The leader training and local strategy processes created a good atmosphere throughout the organization. The entirely understandable and somewhat hesitant attitude that I had noted on my first tour of the American SAS kingdom was replaced by enthusiasm. The fear was even gone at the freight terminal in New York. Instead, there was peace, accord, and continual focus on improvements with regard to our most important goals: security, punctuality, and service. After about six months, it became clear that everyone was on the same page as to what was important for the entire organization.

Punctuality became the key indicator of our success. Delays were extremely rare. Both passengers and cargo arrived when they should, and the planes went back to Europe on schedule. Eventually, we also began receiving very good feedback from customers. That is, perhaps, the strongest evidence that a turnaround is starting to work. And last but not least: revenue rose and costs went down. SAS and profitability merged in the United States.

Angelika and the boys gradually settled in. We had a house in Connecticut with a very large garden and all modern conveniences. But they missed our house and friends in Norway. My career still ruled most of their lives. It was the way it was. We discussed options to a small extent, for they were not sure it was practical that I continue with SAS. One advantage was that I earned enough that we didn't have to worry about the family finances. Rental income for our house in Norway and only token rent in the United States meant that we were able to pay off a large part of our house mortgage, laying the groundwork for increased freedom of movement later. It helped to think of the situation as an investment.

In the beginning of 1985, we rented an entire conference center in Long Island to collect all the threads from the strategy process through a kick-off meeting with all employees in what we now call The New Eastern Area. The area actually covered less than half the North American continent geographically but accounted for nearly 80 percent of the activity of SAS in the United States. Later, we intended to do a similar event for our people on the West Coast and in my old area, Chicago and the Midwest.

I remember being more excited than nervous. I felt well prepared because what I was saying was as much from me as from the company. I had already lived with the content for several years during turnaround operations at headquarters in Stockholm and SAS Cargo Norway, and I didn't have to "act" enthusiastically. I knew that it worked. The only challenge was adapting the rhetoric used, but that was no problem since I had spent over five years in Chicago and New York.

I had stapled the manuscript for my speech into a booklet that everyone would receive. In reality, it was my own edition of *Janne's Little Red Book*, created specifically for The New Eastern Area. It was bound in gray in acknowledgment that red might not sit well in the United States, even though China and the United States had achieved somewhat of a reconciliation due to Nixon's visit to Beijing in 1972; and the blue title, *You Make the Difference*, reminded people a little about the Chinese sovereign's main gospel.

Since I aimed my main message directly at the individual, I also needed to have a personal starting point. If you want to reach an individual in the organization, there is no use speaking in the third person about what the company offers and expects from the individual. It is only by using *you, me,* and *us* that you can reach them, especially in the United States. Thus, there was only one way to go:

This is an important opportunity for me to meet each and every one of you to discuss the opportunities and challenges that lie ahead in The New Eastern Area. We are moving into a new era, and we in the East probably have the best opportunities to take advantage of changes now taking place. Our geographical location, the economic situation in the eastern area, and the high competence and effort you have recently made give us a solid competitive advantage. We all have good reason to be optimistic and have great faith in our success—and in the success of SAS in the beginning of 1985.

The main reason for this is the success in this room: *You make the difference.* This is not another empty phrase or slogan. It is the simple truth. Why? Because the most important thing in any business is the people who interact with other people. This appeals to our external relationships such as travel agents, corporate travel offices, and our passengers. And, equally important, internally in the company, between us: between individuals and departments, between The Eastern Area and Stockholm Headquarters. None of this would work without each and every one of us in this room, prepared and willing as we are to communicate, to help each other solve problems, to work together and for ourselves.

The new organization is useful and purposeful, but an organization chart in and of itself lacks value. It is our participation in the organization that has meaning. It is you who create our product and its quality. That is why you are so important.

Now, when I look at this speech, I feel as though I might have missed my calling as an evangelist. But I had actually tapped into the very heart of the audience's mood thanks to the thorough work we had done with the whole company and all the employees throughout 1984. Of course, I had run the content past some of my coworkers. They believed just as wholly and firmly in what I said as I did. That, of course, was a prerequisite for the 400 employees who were in the audience to believe.

The process also showed that customers and employees value simple human factors most. Undoubtedly, that is what also creates job satisfaction internally and externally. That was the basis for the six main points in the SAS philosophy on which I continued my speech.

1. The most important thing for a human being is to know that s/he is needed.

2. Satisfied customers and employees are worth more than the billions of dollars in aircraft.

3. All—both customers and employees—want and deserve to be treated as individuals. That is what good service is all about: to meet the needs and expectations of both customers and employees at every point of contact.

4. Freeing people from rigid control through instruction, policy provisions, and orders—giving individuals freedom to be responsible for their own ideas, decisions, and actions—is to release hidden resources that would otherwise be unavailable, both for the individual and for the company.

5. A person cannot take responsibility without being informed. An informed person cannot help but take responsibility.

6. If you need proof that this is a reality in SAS philosophy, take a look at where we invest the most money.

The whole turnaround in SAS centrally and in the United States showed that people were the company's greatest value because a plane trip is primarily a product in which the human factor matters most to customers and because the people represent the biggest investment.

Some of the message was addressed as much to the managers as to the employees. It is important to obligate the managers when all those vested in the company hear and see it. Then the workers have the opportunity to correct their managers, which is a sign of a confident and learning organization. In fact, it happened at its best during the turnaround at SAS in the United States.

For the rest of the speech, I concentrated on the corporation's new strategy: marketing, sales, distribution, logistics, and production would continue in the same direction toward which we had intensely worked during the central and local strategy work, and through the management-training program:

> Everything we do—and do *not* do—shall be evaluated and measured up against company and customer results, not just activities and volume.

One afternoon, I was invited to the Teamsters hangout. It was a tradition I had never heard of but proved to be an honor for a leader. The significance? The top manager deserved an award for working together with a union to achieve a shared goal: a goal benefiting both union members and the company. I received a gift, and the union insisted that the whole evening was on them.

We managed to continue to focus on the job of evaluating and following up and found more and more new ways of working. Thinking outside the box and sharing good ideas with others were no longer uncommon practices. Met with skepticism on my first tour, I now took pleasure in traveling around to the various stations and departments.

Interestingly, it was not only revenues that had increased. In several areas, there were reduced costs because all expenses were now evaluated based on whether they helped to achieve our goals. During the first process of cost cutting, put in place in 1982, we cut costs in areas where the opportunity to increase earnings was destroyed because there was no coherent strategy behind the reductions.

I was welcomed like royalty in many places. The Americans' ability to idolize individuals is enormous. I could not help delighting in the results and, after a while, felt a bit like a guru. It is impossible not to be influenced by hero worship, no matter how much you try to keep your feet on the ground. The one who noticed that most was Angelika. Fortunately, she was also not afraid to speak up when I flew a little too high.

After only two years in the United States, I was called in to see one of the deputy chief executive officers at headquarters in Stockholm. He was full of praise for what we had accomplished "over there." The increased traffic with both passengers and freight to and from North America had generated additional traffic and increased profitability on the other SAS routes as well—in addition to the effect of the main turnaround operation in the company that was still in progress.

But there was one country that still lagged behind and where SAS had not seen the full benefits of the process. That was Norway—despite the fact that its economy was then going through tremendous growth. The credit market was deregulated. Money gushed like a geyser not only from oil and gas activities in the North Sea, but also from all kinds of land-based businesses. We were at the beginning of what was later called the Norwegian yuppie era and what afterward would cause both banks and other financial institutions to shake almost to their foundations. But near the end of 1985, no one knew how it was going to end. What mattered now was exploiting the upsurge. As The Businessman's Airline, SAS wanted its piece of the action.

I knew immediately where the CEO was headed with the conversation, but I had no desire to move back to Norway. I wanted to enjoy my success in the United States a while longer and enjoy myself as long as I could in my little royal box. I could probably remain there a year or two more if I absolutely wanted to and was certainly not *ordered* home to Norway. Yet I understood the message when I left the spacious office and the chief executive said, "If I were you, I would take the job in Norway."

During my going away party in New York, the Teamsters again made their presence known. They rented a large hall and invited all the employees. When the formal part of the program began, I was placed in a chair on the dance floor where an unknown woman suddenly came swinging out to some provocative music. She was presented as the airline's newest employee and the best telephone salesperson we ever had.

She was none of that, of course, although she was definitely professional. She waltzed around me as she removed one garment after another. It was impossible not to be embarrassed, but when I saw that everyone was bursting with excitement, I could not help but find it funny. Afterward I learned that this was also a Teamsters tradition and another expression of forthright confidence.

The head of the union then spoke warmly about how we had worked together to develop SAS into a healthy and respectable workplace. I received a gold-plated brick engraved with "And the Bricks Came Tumbling Down." I heard that SAS had been a tough nut to crack for the Teamsters. They previously had not received any of the cooperation they desired. With the new management, the barriers—"The Bricks"—between employees and management fell.

After this party, I felt it was time to go home. My balloon was probably still filled with hero helium when I thought I had met the toughest union men through the Teamsters leaders in the United States. Cadillacs, black leather coats, and other Mafia attributes notwithstanding, they would prove to be pussycats compared to the trade union movement that met me at home in Norway: a 12-headed troll whose demands and ability for flexibility seemed initially like it was chiseled right out of Norwegian bedrock.

9

"ROCKWOOL-LAYER"— THE INVISIBLE HURDLE

I probably still felt a bit like a king when I assumed the managing director role at SAS Headquarters at Oslo Airport on January 1, 1986. In addition, Norwegian business was on its way to an *all-time high* with stock prices and stock volume that no one had seen the likes of since World War I. Large publicly traded industrial companies, such as Borregaard and Kosmos, were in the game. There was economic movement and growth on all sides after the housing and real estate markets were deregulated early in the 1980s, and later the credit market.

Banks poured money into one castle in the air after another. Investment enthusiasm was great, and big money was invested in the most unbelievable projects. Norwegian Polar Navigation, Media Vision, VIP Scandinavia, Sim-X: companies that still send financial chills up the spines of those that threw themselves on the bandwagon. Six-liter bottles of champagne were downed on the Barock Stock Exchange. It was "Happy Børsday"[1] every day.

---

[1] Literally "Happy Exchange Day," a play on words in Norwegian. *Børs* is "the stock exchange" in Norway so *børsdag* (exchange day) and *bursdag* (birthday) would sound similar in Norwegian.

Mentioning moderation and possible decline was like spitting against the wind. There was no room for skeptics and sourpusses.

For the Norwegian managing director of The Businessman's Airline, it should have been a simple matter of tapping into this apparently insatiable market, but it was not. Of course we took advantage of every opportunity to quickly sell flights and air cargo; but the Norwegian organization, which was to provide all of this, had not yet adapted to the new reality. Both commercially and within SAS, the effects of the first turnaround had begun to slow down. New organizational challenges stood in line.

In fact, the problems were considerably larger than I had imagined. As head of the business in the United States, I had been somewhat sheltered from the rest of SAS. I daresay I quickly returned to reality once I left the US. Norway was a long way from the gilded bricks and cheerful abuse I received from twinkling Teamsters representatives. I understood very quickly why I had little or no choice but to take this new job: there was a lot to do here.

From a marketing perspective, SAS was still a success. All the new products were in place: EuroClass and tourist class on European routes; first business class and tourist class on long-haul routes. By 1982, the company was already starting to earn a profit again. That continued and increased in 1983 when SAS received the Airline of the Year award. From a business perspective, 1984 was even better.

Perhaps the results came a little too quickly. I think people had developed a sense that everything was back to normal before they had time to consider the new market situation and before lasting changes were firmly in place in the organization. That was particularly true of the leaders who had been less involved in the turnaround; yet it seemed as if coworkers in the operational links were again starting to lean a little too much on the old success syndrome. As if the company had only experienced a few passing snow flurries—not that much of the snow that the company had previously plowed away was, in fact, about to melt.

The danger was far from over. We had only reached the first target: getting the company back in the black. Perhaps we had not been clever enough communicating that this goal was only the first step on the road toward more long-term and bigger goals—as Carlzon had outlined in his *Little Red Book*, but which had possibly drowned a little in the hails of profits and success.

Milestones are important to celebrate, but they can quickly become a pillow if they are not made the starting point for new goals. This book's coauthor has climbed several of the highest mountains in the world. He always says it inevitably goes downhill from the top. The happiest moments come when you are so high that you are positive you are going to reach the top, but you haven't yet begun to worry about the trip down. As soon as the initial euphoria has settled follows the feeling "What now?" unless you have already set new goals and realize the summit is but another step along the way.

Based on my experience in the business world, I tend to agree. The difference, though, is that downturns in the business world can be much more brutal than coming down in one piece from a high mountain. You need to establish and lay the foundations for new goals on the way up—jumping the curve, so to speak. In practice, that means finding the right point on the company's development curve that creates new growth. Every product and every service has a shelf life. You need to think fresh and define how the business will survive the future while you still have freedom of choice and action—and can still take advantage of the drive that is available while on the upward journey. When the curves are beginning to point downward and existing products and services are about to reach their best-before date, it is usually too late to turn back. Before you know it, your back is against the wall and there is only one remedy— the one most leaders resort to under pressure situations: cut costs everywhere.

That was what they had started with at SAS before Carlzon arrived in 1980 and the first red figures were beginning to show up in the financial statements. The first cost cutting in 1982 was a paper exercise rather than a learning process. Admittedly, the employees had been involved, but without a clear business philosophy of where and how they were going to earn and spend the money, the cost cuts were random. When the new strategy for The Businessman's Airline was in place at the beginning of 1981, we saw that we had proposed cuts in the wrong areas when we should have strengthened our efforts in line with strategic guidance.

When the strategy was put in place to control the level of income and expenses, we saw that the actual cost consequence was in making an extra investment of 260 million Swedish kronor: that was contrary to what many had thought and believed necessary. This investment was the key to new success. Internally, though, it may have helped to reinforce the impression that the company had not actually been in a financial crisis. How could a company that looked like it was heading off a cliff afford to cough up a quarter of a billion crowns?

The analyses also showed that we needed to reduce costs by 20-25 percent in the long term to preserve competitiveness in a market under constant pressure. That would not be possible without significant involvement of both managers and employees. How could we create awareness of that when the company seemed to be in such good shape again? And how could we accomplish it without doing it at the expense of our major priorities: safety, punctuality, and service?

During the first part of the turnaround—1981 to 1984—we felt we had cohesion and everyone and everything was headed in the same direction. Without new and clear mutual goals, groups of employees began to set their own goals, aided by trade unions and middle managers who had no ownership of the processes. Eventually the organization spread in different directions—not the one we had tried to get everyone to concentrate on for three years: the market and the customer's best interests.

The pilots and technicians wanted new aircrafts, which many competing companies had acquired. Instead, we had sold the new aircrafts we had purchased because they did not fit in our new and profitable route net, and we now had quite a number of aging planes. In our opinion, they were still completely capable of meeting company requirements for safety, punctuality, and passenger demands for comfort. The pilots and technical personnel believed the planes were old-fashioned and could affect safety. It did not help when Carlzon stated: "We will never buy new planes so the pilots can have new cockpits to sit in or engineers can have new planes to play with. We will not purchase new planes until they add value to our business travelers and, thus, make us more competitive."

That was like pouring fuel on the fire. Did the puffed-up CEO think that the pilots and technicians *played* at work? The old struggle between professional and technical people on the one side, and the market and customers on the other side flared up again. Previously, the technical department had been king in the organization and received most of the attention. They were accustomed to getting approval for their demands. Now they began to rattle their sabers to retake the throne, first with arguments regarding maintenance and punctuality. When that did not impress leadership, they began to argue about safety.

We were doomed to lose the discussion. It escalated so far that it ended up on the front pages of newspapers in

Norway, Sweden, and Denmark. Of course, we were on the defensive. The combination of "old planes" and "poor safety" was obvious, especially when the information was based on reviews from sources within the company. Carlzon took reporters on flights and visits to workshops to try to correct the impression. We received international declarations that safety at SAS was never behind other airlines. Fortunately, this didn't affect traffic, but we still felt pushed into a defensive position.

Other groups in the company also jumped on the discontent bandwagon. At the time, SAS had over 30 trade unions in the three owner countries. Now the demands came one after another for new wage levels, better arrangements for free travel, meals, holidays, working hours, as well as a number of other conditions that might have been on hold for the last three years when a common volunteer spirit had existed. In our defensive situation and in fear of destroying what was left of the good SAS spirit—destruction of which would spill over to the customers' experience—we accepted many of the demands, until we realized that no one wins a battle sitting in the corner of the ring. Which demands should *we* make?

It was in this situation that we learned the depth of our blunder by not involving middle management in the initial stage of the turnaround. By sidelining middle managers and moving much of the responsibility out to the operational part of the organization, we had overlooked the latent power in uniting everyone toward a common goal and had given away our long-standing options of instructing and controlling.

Some leaders had intuitively understood that they needed to engage in the process. They had converted their previous administrative and controlling features to actually leading and following up with their coworkers so they were better able to exercise their new responsibilities. This is what we had come a long way toward accomplishing in the United States and SAS Cargo Norway, where we had involved the middle managers through leadership training programs.

However, many middle managers had experienced the turnaround as a time of slaughter. All of a sudden, their positions were almost without content, and they neither understood nor received help to understand how they could contribute to converting those positions to functions that could benefit the new strategy. Therefore, they moved over to the sidelines, where they contributed as little as possible. So it goes with managers and coworkers who are not involved—sometimes not even noticed. Everyone wants to do a good job; but if no one sees you, it is often difficult to know what you can contribute. That type of energy is dangerous to have running around the organization, for it can suddenly turn on you.

That is what happened. Now they knew what they had and came back in full force. Their own nebulous state helped the emerging discontent and opposition to grow. Not that they actively opposed the leadership. That wasn't necessary. In the organizational vacuum that had arisen due to indistinct goals and a new common direction, growth conditions were present for all sorts of subcultures.

Carlzon also acknowledged that it had been a mistake to skip over the middle management layer. In his book *Moments of Truth*, published in 1985, he tells about an episode where he came from the United States to Stockholm and passengers were running around looking for their baggage. The reason? The screens displaying where luggage could be found were black. When Carlzon went to the information desk and suggested to the person behind the counter that some temporary signs be used, he was told:

> "That's exactly what I think! The system broke down last week, and I said to the manager that we had to set up some makeshift signs, so people can find their baggage. But he said that it would soon be repaired, so it wasn't necessary."
>
> "But that was a whole week ago?"
>
> "That's exactly what I said! But the boss said that now it had been a whole week, so now it *had* to be repaired soon."

Back in the office, Carlzon contacted the station's division chief and asked that he notify the appropriate boss that he could either move his desk down to the arrival hall where he could personally experience the problems and make decisions based on them, or delegate the necessary decisions to those who worked there. Carlzon summed up the situation:

This little story illustrates one of the major problems in SAS today, what has internally come to be called "the Rockwool-layer." This boss had not understood that his role had changed. His new task was to set the objectives for how information and the rest of the business in the arrival hall should function, then delegate responsibility to those who work in the hall. He was not to sit in his office and make decisions about signs.

The girl's conduct also shows how hard it is to get the new thinking to penetrate. Why did she mention it at all? She saw the problem and understood how to resolve it. Nevertheless, she wouldn't risk taking responsibility. She felt that the boss would be angry if she did something without asking for permission: it requires courage to incur the boss's disapproval deliberately. Therefore, she chose the safe way—she delegated upward.

For my part, I could add that neither the girl nor her boss had received sufficient opportunities to practice our new working methods. It was not *they* but *we* in top management who had created the Rockwool-layer because we had not run a more thorough and inclusive process.

There was nothing wrong with the philosophy or strategy behind the new initiative in SAS. The problem was that it had not reached the whole organization. Thus, more and more employees fell back to the old thought and action patterns. Without mutual development processes where every team in the organization has the same picture of the direction, it is impossible to get everyone to go the same way. In a business that would soon have 35,000 people, of which 20,000 were original employees in the SAS airline, there could be large divergence if people begin to go their own ways, especially when lack of understanding is on the middle management level—as it was at this time at SAS.

The middle managers were not capable of leading their coworkers in the right direction. There were no systems for sanctions. An employee who neither receives rewards for appropriate behavior nor recriminations for unwanted behavior will automatically act more and more at his or her sole discretion. The business can, of course, limp along; most people have the will and ability to do their best, as with the girl in the arrival hall at the Stockholm airport. But it can also progress in the wrong direction, as in the former situation in the airport terminal in New York, where I was the one who made a fool of myself.

This was typical of what I encountered at Oslo Airport in the beginning of 1986. As Norway's managing director, I got closer to the business in Denmark and Sweden. We put a number of processes in place—meetings with the different departments and trade unions—where friction was highest. One of the measures for bringing out discontent was asking everyone to list everything that was bad and everything that was good. The result was consistently 5:95, the opposite of what we had thought. The problem was that the five bad things overshadowed all the good things.

Then we tried to restore the new operational responsibility by making management responsible for correcting the 5 percent that made people unhappy, while the employees continued to be responsible for the 95 percent with which they were pleased.

I think the two biggest challenges at SAS Norway were to get all of management and the trade unions on board. I started with the unions, as I did in the United States, and invited them to an afternoon meeting. My first goal was to find out what their formal demands and possible causes of discontent were, and then create a mood and loosen their collars with pizza and beer.

It was nothing like the scary people in black Cadillacs and ankle-length leather coats. Nevertheless, I experienced similar feelings of powerlessness when I met a multiheaded monster of leaders of 12 small and large unions. Whereas the Teamsters leaders emerged as cooperative and streamlined, from the onset this was a gang of skeptical and uncooperative power-hungry people who sat with daggers drawn and, to some extent, conflicting interests. Some seemed as keen to throw dirt at each other as at the leadership. Some wondered later on if serving pizza and beer was a plan to corrupt them. If that was the case, then I should understand that Norwegian trade unions were "untouchable," contrary to what I had been accustomed to in the United States.

Behind the newfound service façade that SAS passengers were experiencing burned an intense flame. It was only a matter of time before customers were impacted. Had I not brought myself down to earth so quickly after my stay in the United States, I think things might have gone sour. Fortunately, though, I had mentally returned to the stack of pallets on which I conducted my first meeting at JFK's cargo terminal. At the same time, I also had nothing to defend.

My role in the central project group was more an advisory one than a decision making one. No one attempted to make me more personally responsible other than the occasional derisive "management," which is highly legitimate toward one who has undertaken a leadership role. When the trade unions attack, it is always wiser to reason that they have something important on their mind and listen to what they have to say.

As people expressed their feelings, the mood eased. Then they were ready for a little partying. Fortunately, no one turned down the food, even if there wasn't much of a party mood. Compared to the initial mood, though, I felt that we had come a long way. Not to mention that I now understood the power and influence held by the various associations. The largest and most influential were the Aviation Functionaries Union, the Workshop Union, and Trade and Business. The Cabin and Pilot Union worked more against the central leadership in SAS.

Management and union face each other most often in two venues. One handles wage negotiations that mostly follow a set pattern. The other handles how we work together on a daily basis. I was most concerned with the latter and decided to try to get the leaders of these three main unions into the extended management group—the Management Forum—which met once a month. That proved to be a wise move. The leader of the Functionaries Union was an especially outstanding leader who understood he had to affect the future for his members, rather than insist on rights from the past. Every now and then we had battles, but most often we found constructive solutions together.

When it came to the trade unions, we made a general mistake with long-lasting repercussions from which SAS still suffers. Rather than use common understanding and good dialogue that eventually developed between the management and employees' representatives to thoroughly go through the agreement and adjust it in line with the current and future work situation and distribution of responsibility, we only performed new patchwork. I'm not thinking primarily of the collective agreements. They were good enough and straightforward enough to negotiate because they related directly to the company's earning ability and general economic situation.

The thing that really stuck—and still does—were the provisions relating to working hours, rest breaks, professional refinements, responsibilities, etc. This agreement was developed and adapted to SAS as a *production* company in a somewhat sheltered competitive situation where the customers were used to paying what it cost when they traveled by air.

We saw and understood the constraints this involved when the company was about to transform itself into an efficient, customer-oriented, and market-adapted organization. Suddenly, there were those who could not perform tasks they naturally could have done. Not because they did not have the time or the opportunity, but because it was beyond their agreed area of responsibility. Because of this, we did not get the flow in the organization to take optimal advantage of all the managers' and workers' resources. Consequently, the new process to cut costs—*Trim 86*—became considerably more difficult than expected. Normally, it would have been easier to cut idle time rather than positions. Such was not to be at SAS.

We began, albeit cautiously, to try to change the agreements in Norway. Yet, without a common strategic approach throughout the whole company, there was never any pressing need. I think it was more a lack of focus and a little cowardice on the part of top management rather than ill will from the unions. Without having revitalized the Rockwool-layer, we perceived the organization as a bit vulnerable, even if the climate was about to get better. Maybe we were too keen on keeping the good climate because it was pleasant. Nevertheless, when work tasks and areas of responsibility were already put into play through the company's customer orientation, we should have pushed the entire process to its final goal, even if it created a little extra noise. That would have been perceived as an ordinary game, not a rematch as later attempts at explaining harmonization were.

The management group in Norway lacked cohesion. It consisted of 22 people who belonged to both the new and old company culture, of which three were union leaders. This made sticking with a standard arrangement for

leadership training unlikely. We had to build a new culture from scratch; in other words, do the job we did not
do with the managers in the first part of the turnaround.
I contacted Professor Willi Railo, who at the time was
Norway's leading performance psychologist. He had
just started the Scandinavian Leadership company along
with five previous consultants from SAS Management
Consultants who had been involved in several parts of
the turnaround in the airline.

Railo had achieved remarkable results as an athlet-
ic coach and performance group coach for the business
world. His simple message of replacing the three impera-
tives "I have to; I ought to; I shall" with "I want to; I dare
to; I can" fit perfectly for what we had tried to achieve in
the entire rank at SAS: individuals would accept the greatest amount of responsibility—no matter what level they
were in the organization. Responsibility is responsibility—regardless of the person, length of service, experience,
or other individual circumstances.

Scandinavian Leadership had developed a mentor
program based on this philosophy. We decided to send
the whole Norwegian management team through it. The
program involved a consultant first observing us for a time
to get a picture of how we practiced our management job
in relation to three main areas: strategic work, administrative tasks, and problem solving. The consultant would
record how much time we spent on each area and how we
performed the tasks in relation to the company's strategic
guidance. The latter part still remained that all priorities

and decisions should be based on whether or not they created profitability in the market—not how they corresponded to the old plans for logistics and production. The results of the observations would then be presented and discussed openly in the management group.

Not everyone was excited about it. Since the most important part of one's leader conduct is to set a good example, we decided that I was going to be the first guinea pig. I ended up with a Finnish psychologist who followed me around for an entire week and registered everything I did. It was a unique experience, especially in the beginning. I was constantly more bothered about whether I did the right things in the right way than about what I actually did. Eventually I forgot that the psychologist was there. He became more like a backdrop, a part of the furniture, whether I was in the office or in meetings.

The feedback wasn't entirely positive but exceedingly beneficial. It turned out that I was good at strategic work but spent too much time on problem solving and administrative tasks that others could have done. And I was not always good at problem solving. For example, when people came to get help and I was really busy, I still let them come in. The result was that I listened to them with half an ear. Both my body and mind told them that they were unwanted. That kind of double communication makes people feel insecure; they are unlikely to come again. Instead, I should have asked them to come back a little later, after I had completed what I was doing, so I could concentrate and be constructive.

This analysis was considerably deeper than the one I had undergone during the leadership development program in the United States, and I have to admit that it was with some trepidation that I watched my strong and weak leadership skills laid out and presented to everyone in the management group. Perhaps it was the last remnants of the American Big Apple bravura that had caused me to go through with this. Regardless, there was not much left of that now, and it was too late to turn back. I had no choice but to lay out the results at the next management meeting.

"Okay, folks—here you see what I am like. Do you think the result is consistent with your experience of the boss? I see some things to work on here, not just for me, but also for you in terms of giving me feedback. Now it's your turn. Who will sign up first?"

Their reception was a bit unexpected. I think I anticipated that they would use my results as a starting point to look inside themselves. Instead, they threw themselves at my weakest qualities, identified in the report, and wanted to "help" me confirm what I needed to work on. Initially, it made me defensive and reinforced the impression that I needed significant coaching—from my coworkers as well. At the same time, their eagerness to correct me reflected back on their own frustration.

Nevertheless, they agreed to go through the same process. When everyone had been through it and we had discussed the results, not only was there more balance in the management team's interaction but also a much greater openness and security. To find the "truth" about oneself can be a tough but necessary experience if one is to be confident enough to lead others.

Similar processes took place in Denmark, Sweden, and other parts of the organization which had not already been through a modernization process, such as the United States, for example. The processes were constantly adapted to different situations in the various regions and departments. Leader and organization development must always be established on basic, common foundations, which reflect the organization's values and strategies. However, the educational approach and methods need to be adapted to those who go through the process. It is not a given that concepts that are successful in one department will work as well in another.

Developing teams and leaders is much more about listening than in forcing people to accept ready-made solutions. All successful leader and organizational development processes of which I have been a part have been tailored. Mass-produced performance projects can provide some short-lived inspiration but rarely with lasting effect.

10

HIGH UP

After about six months, the process began to produce results both in Norway and at the corporate level. I noticed that we increasingly spoke the same language, and controversies were no longer just about goals but about means. That is an important difference. Disagreement is valuable, but not when expressed in the form of persistent battles concerning already-established goals. Discussions about the best paths to those goals, or whether the goals should be adjusted or reevaluated, are important.

We never got that far—quite the opposite, in fact. As the entire management team grasped the same picture of the goals, there was only enthusiasm. While we spent many of the first management meetings discussing limitations and problems, which probably influenced my prioritization of problem solving between management meetings, we now discussed opportunities and solutions on how we would reach both goals: increase revenues and reduce costs in the targeted areas.

With such clear guidance, it was suddenly quite easy to move the process out to the organization. We drew up clear responsibility and authority areas. Most managers no longer had a problem understanding the importance of moving most of the responsibility as far down the ladder as possible. It was also easy to keep track of the results with our new budgeting and financial reporting systems put in place during the first part of the turnaround. Now we could determine what we earned per passenger as well as per kilo in shipping.

We worked on small and large efficiency projects everywhere. There was uneven traffic of cargo and passengers at smaller airports, yet different personnel were allocated to serve freight customers and passenger customers. Consequently, we created a common counter where all personnel could serve both passengers and cargo customers. In some places, we combined the ticket counter with check-in. Thus, customers didn't have to stand in two lines and we reduced personnel costs at the same time.

Real organizational development and follow-up took place as a result of logical thought processes where it became easy to check if we were on the right path:

Organizational development

Process	Results
★ How do we function as a team?	★ Have we reached our goals?
★ How do we review our efforts?	★ What is our contribution?
★ How satisfied are we?	★ How can we be better?

So we can:	So SAS can:
★ Feel free	★ Be the first choice for business travelers
★ Accept responsibility	★ Maintain an acceptable market share
★ Actively influence	★ Renew and expand our fleet

This was a new way of working. SAS had previously coordinated five-year plans and forecasted development five years in the future but devoted little time to ensure that the company was on track. Now we broke all the goals down into measurable factors that we could easily check. The requirement for regularity was 99 percent. In practice, that meant we only accepted atrocious weather conditions and unpredictable technical incidents as reasons for cancellations. Punctuality improved, and we continued to work actively on it.

The requirement was that 80 percent of planes would take off within 2 minutes of the published departure time, 90 percent within 10 minutes. This was very ambitious at the time but not unrealistic. In some periods, we were ahead of our goals. We thoroughly analyzed all deviations. When the cause for delay was neither weather nor technical related, we looked for solutions to prevent any recurrence. We thus discovered where the organization still had weaknesses, while at the same time creating increased accountability by those who performed the tasks.

The level of service on board and on the ground improved, especially after the cabin crew took part in determining what they could manage over various routes. For example, now they served full breakfasts with hot rolls in the morning between Oslo and Copenhagen, and managed a round with the drink wagon and duty-free items before the plane landed. At the time, the latter meant much more than it does today because passengers did not have access to duty-free shops on arrival.

We analyzed how long passengers thought it acceptable to wait at the airport at ticket and check-in counters before they could board the plane. Employees even made suggestions on how to decrease wait times. Some of the solutions included better interaction with other units and correct information given to passengers. Business travelers, especially, were concerned about this. They would rather arrive at the airport and go directly to the plane just before it took off. Targets were set so that 90 percent of the business class passengers wouldn't have to wait more than 5 minutes. In tourist class, 90 percent of the passengers need only wait 15 minutes.

Handling time for luggage from the time the plane landed until it was on the conveyor belt was set to 20 minutes. In practice, that meant passengers never had to wait more than 10 minutes for their luggage. Many people think it is the airport that determines this time, but this is something the airlines can influence based on crew size and the kind of logistics they have on the ground. For example, Singapore Airlines' practice is that luggage should be on the conveyor belt by the time passengers get to baggage claim—no matter where in the world they are. And at SAS we set in place additional goals for management regarding delayed, damaged, and lost luggage.

In addition to the measures taken for business travelers, we set in motion projects to increase traffic in cargo and tourism. Our thinking was that when the company had achieved sufficient sustainability with full-fare passengers, we could obtain additional revenue by filling up available capacity with no additional expense. That's always good business.

The danger of focusing intensely on daily work methods and short-term results is that you can lose sight of long-term goals, the important seed that ensures future earnings. Therefore, we created some working groups (management groups) consisting of selected managers and employees.

The largest working group was the Management Forum for Action Planning, which also had three elected union officials. Its main task was to follow up on organizational development and leadership. We had made what we called the CAC process—Culture Architecting and Coaching. The most important goals in this group were

- exchanging information between business areas and top management
- sharing experiences through dialogue and discourse
- managing disputes—what has not been done and why?
- planning new measures
- providing individual coaching on all levels

We also laid down some basic management principles, where it was written that SAS management is to

- work for other people's success
- be the team's coach
- facilitate decentralized decisions
- give constructive feedback
- listen

- lead with a good example
- be a leader, not a boss

The basic philosophy was "management by love" rather than "management by fear," which had characterized parts of the old control regime. As a result, we also said, "It is better to ask for forgiveness than to ask for permission." With this as a guide, the young woman Carlzon met in the arrival hall would never have asked her boss if she should put up a makeshift sign. She would have just done it. The boss might never have noticed it.

In order to follow up on the leader principles, we initiated leadership development programs at all levels, as well as new courses in service and interaction for all who had contact with customers. All employees received career planning counseling, as well as a host of other things to make employment at SAS even more attractive. Our philosophy was simple:

- Happy employees create happy customers.
- The best people attract the best customers.

The basic line of thinking was that we primarily create success through people. We do this through an organizational culture characterized by

- trust
- opportunities
- change

In an organization influenced strongly by technical focus, it took time before everyone managed to accept this. Some had trouble accepting that new aircraft and other technical devices in themselves would not make it more attractive to fly with SAS. Yet these values opened the way for new thinking, also when it came to technical areas. The new thinking was, as Carlzon had tried to express, that we should consider all purchases and expenses from a holistic customer perspective—that is, whether or not it contributes to more satisfied customers and more profitability per customer.

The argument for this line of thinking was the same as the base values in all customer care:

- It is the customers who pay our salary.
- Customers have demands on us; we have none on them.

In practice, that would mean that if the customers demand new aircraft in order to travel with us and they pay full price, then they'll get it. If we need bigger planes to meet the demands of increased traffic on some routes, then we purchase them. We do whatever the market and customers demand at all times. Eventually I think it hit home with most. Now, when proposals were made for technical innovations, they were most often justified by the market. Even the trade unions' proposals often contained more regard for the customers than for the company's employees.

There was also a lot of activity on the market side. Our new customer perspective was about to take root

on the passenger side just as much as the thinking behind Egil Budde's amazing salmon stunt in New York
had attached itself to the cargo departments. We were
creating a hothouse of growth in the United States to
help Norwegian companies that wanted to enter the US
market.

We gathered national and local participants from
the business and political world at a two-day seminar in
Northern Norway to discuss how we could create greater
growth in that part of the country.

We arranged exclusive high-level business confer-
ences in our conference center in Oslo and invited 30-35
guests where renowned international speakers opened dialogue and observations.

We introduced and presented business awards for
innovation and other successes.

In summary, we positioned ourselves exactly where
we wanted to be as engaged contributors in the social are-
na. We gained a lot of goodwill, both in the market and
with the government, who was our Norwegian owner
who laid the framework for much of our business.

At this point in time, SAS was so popular that it was
ranked as the best company to work for in all of Scandinavia. "Everyone" wanted to work for SAS, regardless of
the position he or she could get. If you told people that
you worked at SAS, you were envied. It was, of course, a
source of inspiration and motivation to push a little hard-
er, but perhaps also a little risky. There are more who end
up flat on their backs in good times than bad.

As a leader, I wanted to give both middle managers and employees the greatest possible freedom to perform their tasks. But since the essence of our business was based on satisfied customers, I also felt that I needed to keep abreast of how things actually were in the customer area. Fortunately, I still traveled a lot, so I had plenty of opportunity to talk with other passengers and SAS employees without looking like I was checking up on them. I checked the cleanliness of the restrooms in our main airports, whether there were enough baggage trolleys in place or if luggage arrived on time, whether we got what we were promised on board, and so on. I could do all of this without employees feeling as though the boss was looking over their shoulder. If I discovered irregularities and need for corrections, I always went the service route through the leaders in the chain so I didn't stymie responsibility.

Sometimes, such as when fog at Oslo Airport prevented any flights from taking off or landing, the management group had our own activities in the departure hall. We brought trolleys with coffee, juice, and rolls, and engaged in conversation with passengers. In such situations, when people were already annoyed because the planes were grounded, it was often easy to discover other sources of dissatisfaction. Of course, it was also an opportunity to reverse the mood, which fortunately we managed most of the time. I daresay that this kind of action from management was considerably more successful than when I tried to deal with the delayed, upset passengers at JFK Airport in New York.

Nevertheless, we also committed the biggest blunders in top management during this period. In 1987, the profit of the entire SAS organization was 120 million USD—and that in a market which, as a whole, still had a deficit. The contribution from Norway was significant. The extremely successful customer orientation whetted appetites for getting a greater piece of the customers' travel-budget pie. So we carved out a new strategy to expand business territory even more: SAS would go from being an airline to a travel company. This locked up the entire journey from the time the customer left his home until he returned.

By 1982, we had basically developed a door-to-door concept for business customers where they could buy tickets and check in for the flight at the hotel. Then upon arrival at the airport, they could go straight to the gate with a printed boarding pass. The arrangement applied to the 20 hotels SAS purchased and managed under its own name.

This was now expanded to picking the customer up at his or her home by airport limousine, and checking in on a mobile terminal in the car where the customer could print out both the boarding passes and luggage tags. The customer, completely checked in, was dropped off at the airport and went straight to the gate or got a free cup of coffee or a drink in the SAS lounge. The driver took care of the luggage. At the other end, the luggage would be on the conveyor when the passenger got to the destination, and a driver waited in the arrival hall to pick up the customer at the appointed place and time. The only thing the traveler had to do was get through customs with his or her luggage.

Market research among our business customers showed that customers wanted this. We even meant to clarify the most important provisions concerning security by the time we launched the product with great fanfare in the beginning of 1986, both internally and in the market. Still the response was lackluster. We did not sell enough of the door-to-door service packages to make it sustainable.

We soon discovered why. We had bypassed the travel agents, still the largest suppliers of flights by far for both business and private sectors. We thought we had such an unbeatable product that we could market, sell, and provide it ourselves. Such thinking backfired on us, causing a backlash. That caused us a lot of grief. Travel agents not only dealt passively with the concept but actively opposed it. At that time, the main income for travel agents was sales commissions from tickets and hotel accommodations. With this deal, there wasn't five cents of revenue. Why would they sell something they didn't make money on? When we tried to get them on board, they weren't very interested. We realized that all hope was lost.

That's how it goes when you forget to involve some of your most important relationships. Perhaps I should have known better after the experience with travel agencies during my apprenticeship in Chicago, even though initially it was the other way around: when I started to take customers away from them, they got on the bandwagon and cooperated. But then, they had the customers first. The door-to-door concept had never been tried by travel agents. We should have brought them on board and let them be part of developing the concept from day one. Now it was too late, so we abandoned the concept as well.

As we neared the end of the 1980s, the air escaped the Norwegian stock market balloon. Bankruptcies came in on a conveyor belt. One major bank after another began to waver. First, the Norwegian Credit Bank (DnC) was put under administration; second, Kreditkassen (CBK); and lastly, Bergen Bank that, through a sneaky maneuver, reportedly bought up the DnC. In reality, it was the opposite in order to camouflage the fact that Bergen Bank had as many skeletons in the closet as the other major Norwegian banks. Shortly after that, Storebrand Insurance Company went over the edge after trying to buy up Skandia in Sweden. In 1986, the offshore industry got hit because of low oil and gas prices. The fish farming industry was still growing, but everyone was more or less affected by these tremors—the airlines market, as well.

Outside Norway's borders, SAS was still very much alive. Both European and intercontinental routes did well. SAS had its main hubs in New York, Bangkok, and Tokyo. South America, Africa, and Australia were left to alliance partners.

Growth often creates need for more growth. For SAS the answer was that it would grow even more—as a travel company. Thus, we made several acquisitions of "strategic positions" in other airline companies and hotel chains.

During 1987 and 1988, SAS bought significant shares in Continental Airlines, LAN Chile, British Midland, and the entire InterContinental hotel chain consisting of 106 hotels. At the same time, we invested large sums of money in the travel data program, Amadeus.

Several questioned how strategic it was to buy all of this. In retrospect, I would say it was a mistake, and in line with the same thinking that forced the door-to-door concept to its knees before it even made it off the ground. We definitely should have been a travel company, but was it right to tie up so much capital by owning everything ourselves? Perhaps we should have signed strategic partnerships and let the core business at SAS continue to grow organically.

The new business concept, now known as SAS Group, was described as follows: "With Europe as a base, the main goal now is to be the best option for the business traveler through effective and integrated air and ground transportation, hotels, airport service, check-in at hotels and airports, and other related services."

The main objective was no less ambitious: "All business areas in SAS shall have a profitable development in a world of increasing competition."

Customer promises were more in line with existing thoughts and practices:

"We're going to make it easier for frequent business travelers to do good business." "We're going to make it easier for travelers to make their vacation the experience of the year."

For the original airline that was still the group's biggest business, the main goal was even more to the point. SAS would now be one of the world's five largest airlines under the motto "One of Five in 95"—that is, one of the world's five largest airlines in 1995. It was ambitious but not impossible, as seen from the development of SAS through the 1980s. In 1988, SAS reached its biggest-ever profit. Operating profit was 2.2 billion NOK (about 339 million USD). With the sale of several planes, it was 3.7 billion NOK (about 570 million USD). Only eight years earlier the company had run a substantial deficit.

If I had been promoted to certain heights during my two years in the United States, it was nothing compared to the honor and glory received by Carlzon. The combination of his first success at the beginning of the 1980s, then publication of a fairly straightforward book that also told where he *had not been* successful, and now results beyond all expectations raised him to heights that no SAS flight would ever attain. And that's where he stayed until he got the boot, so to speak, by the chairman during a TV broadcast in 1993, after many competitors caught up to and flew past SAS.

The Leadership Weekly Newspaper in Norway (*Ukeavisen Ledelse*) commented on Carlzon in 2008 after a lecture he held in Norway at the management school's annual conference. There he told what happened:

> I carried out one good strategy at SAS: I listened to people. Later, I developed a bad strategy. That happened because I was no longer ready to listen. I was too good. My success had made

me less inclined to listen critically to the market and to the employees. I ran the company based on my own needs, and that is
dangerous.

Carlzon felt that his own management philosophy
from the '80s was still current. Admittedly, he had to leave
SAS in 1993 after his visionary strategies had failed. But according to him, the reason the strategies did not work was
that he didn't follow his own management philosophy.

I have always had great respect for what Carlzon did
with SAS and believe he was subjected to a great injustice
when he was forced to leave the company in such a hu-
miliating way. In retrospect, however, I think that it was
around 1988 that SAS really began its long and painful
decline.

It *is* right to jump the curve when you are on the
way up. The question is just whether the leap to "One of
Five in 95" was too much for a company that had only
recently grown out of childhood diseases. All of a sudden, SAS was going to compete aggressively against the
very biggest and best in the industry—at the same time
that the company had spread itself into several other
business areas where it had also tied up a lot of capital.
It is hard to win a war if you have to fight hard on all
fronts at the same time, which today's toughest competitor in the Norwegian market, Norwegian Air, has also
experienced.

It might be tempting to say that I was ready to change
jobs because I saw what was going to happen to SAS, but

that wasn't my reason. I would have at least given notice before looking for something else. In retrospect, I may have sensed that everything was not quite as it should be since I was not unwilling to listen to other job opportunities when the offer from Wilhelmsen came.

Perhaps it was as simple as the thought that my apprenticeship days were over and I had learned what I could learn in the airline industry. Although there were still challenges at SAS both in Scandinavia and internationally, and I had received hints from some corners that some could see me as the new CEO of SAS, more and more often I had a feeling that I was spinning my wheels.

Leaders should probably heed such a danger signal. The day a leader is no longer driven by curiosity and a desire to learn, no longer feels any *aspiration to reach for the top* as a force or a hunger inside, is barely able to summon much attention and enthusiasm for any goals, that leader inflicts those lackluster feelings on the rest of the team. The energy of a management team will always be a mirror image of the top manager's degree of engagement, or lack thereof.

Lack of enthusiasm spreads quickly out to the ranks. When you're sailing, lack of enthusiasm can be compared to a lack of wind. You need to work constantly to take advantage of the wind and provide "that little extra" which imparts a feeling of accomplishment. If the wind (or enthusiasm) begins to taper off or is lost, you will be tempted to find other things to do on board. Before you know it, you just lie there and drift.

Even though I was ripe for change, it still took me a long time to decide to take the job as CEO of Wilhelmsen Lines.

These last few years, I have thought a lot about what really went wrong with SAS. I think it goes considerably deeper than Carlzon being a little high on his horse. I also must acknowledge taking responsibility for some of those errors. The biggest mistake was that we did not dare to take a basic stand on wage settlements and other conditions that were unsustainable in the future. The financial situation of the company was so dire that we could probably have generated understanding for caution. With deregulation of the industry, we understood that low-cost companies would come. When it came to salaries, working hours, and other conditions, we should, therefore, have harmonized all our agreements in order to withstand the adaptations to new cost levels, or, at the very least, produced a common union strategy and common agreements for Denmark, Norway, and Sweden.

The most likely reason it was not done was that we were afraid it would have an adverse effect on employee motivation, resulting in conflicts. We thought since everything was about to improve, why should we upset the applecart? That was naïve and defensive. What would have happened if we had to tighten our finances because development went the other way? Things would have been no better then. It is never the right time to make unpopular decisions. Therefore, one could just as well say it is always the right time. Lesson learned: you need to make essential decisions when you see they are necessary, not wait for a suitable time. That time rarely, if ever, comes.

As one of Carlzon's close coworkers throughout the entire restructuring processes, I could certainly have been better at recognizing the danger signals. A king who stands alone on the mound will, in the end, always be in a position of attack because many people want to tear him down rather than help him, while at the same time he feels invincible. Conversely, I don't know if any of us in the management group would have been able to stop anyone who drove away from the team at such great speed and who lived less and less according to the principles he himself preached. Most of us were probably along for the ride instead of trying to slow the pace.

Along with Carlzon, many of the best professionals of the company's leadership disappeared. Many new ones with little or no aviation experience were appearing. They had no history with the successful turnaround operations of the 1980s under their belts. Their attitude was that *everything* the all-powerful CEO Carlzon had done was under scrutiny. That is a common misconception—pouring the baby out with the bathwater when large changes are required. In this case, it was more the other way around; they should have saved much of the water after the baby was taken out. No managers make exclusively bad or good decisions.

Everyone who has followed the tragic developments in what once was the world's best airline knows the rest of the story. Instead of analyzing what was good and what was bad, the new management began with traditional cost-cutting measures everywhere rather than cutting where it would hurt most in the short term but would give the company better sustainability: personnel costs and working conditions.

Of course, it affected products. The successful and very profitable concepts—EuroClass and first business class that really gave full-fare passengers value for money—were watered down. Meanwhile, the company threw itself into competition with the new budget airlines—a move doomed to fail with the high-cost level SAS had then—and still has.

At the same time, what had been the company's competitive advantage slowly became increasingly larger brake pads. The three-part ownership between Sweden, Denmark, and Norway had literally given SAS a "flying start" during the first two to three post–war decades. The corporate headquarters was located in Stockholm. Copenhagen Airport–Kastrup was made the main airport hub for Scandinavia, which was adapted to fit the market and the people's flight habits. While the commercial center of gravity moved more and more toward Norway and Gardermoen, which is now the busiest airport in Scandinavia, more and more decisions came from Stockholm as they clung to the hope that Copenhagen could still be the main hub. It is still one of the company's curses. Other companies have grabbed many direct flights from Oslo and other Norwegian airports, but SAS still retains Copenhagen as the central hub, even when Hamburg, for example, is only half an hour farther south.

The two worst misjudgments occurred when SAS took over deficit-plagued Braathens in 2002. The first basic mistake was to give the employees from the two companies different wages based on antiquated history that SAS would lead and Braathens would follow. In practice, it meant that people with the same seniority working side by side on inland routes got different wages for the same job. This didn't exactly promote a team spirit on board.

The second mistake was to toss out Braathens' new contract partner, Norwegian Air Shuttle, which emanated out of Busy Bee. Busy Bee flew some of the same routes as SAS's business partner, Widerøe. Bjørn Kjos owned Busy Bee.

Kjos and his gang of old fighter pilot friends from the military, some childhood friends, and a few skilled attorneys from the law firm that Kjos had managed for several years started the Norwegian Air Shuttle with a clean slate and nearly empty pockets. As a consequence, they had to operate as cheaply as possible, which a short time later benefited customers in the form of considerably lower prices and a completely different flexibility.

When SAS took over Braathens, management refused to renew the contract with Norwegian Air Shuttle, figuring it was the end of the line for Kjos and company. But before they knew it, the Braathens plucked hen suddenly became the fox in the Scandinavian henhouse. With a few rented Boeing 737 planes, Norwegian Air began to cater to what previously had been a monopoly of the Norwegian market by the merged SAS and Braathens, and where there had been no emphasis on price. The new company offered flights below 50 percent on the same routes.

Although prices have leveled out in many areas and Kjos is now fighting on nearly all fronts at the same time, Norwegian Air has walked off with most of the fairy-tale growth that has been in aviation in Norway in recent years, both domestically and abroad. SAS should definitely have had a piece of that growth. Norwegian Air's progress is actually based on SAS's inability to adapt to passengers' needs and travel patterns. SAS passengers still have to stop over in Copenhagen to get to many of Europe's most important destinations, while Norwegian Air flies them directly—at prices SAS rarely can match.

Unfortunately, with the cost level and the sluggishness that still seems to characterize the company, and their endless wavering between different concepts, I fear any growth is far off.

11

NEW JOB—OLD CULTURE

Before I boarded the gangway to Wilh. Wilhelmsen's old-fashioned offices in one of the most prestigious locations in Oslo on May 1, 1990, I had had meetings with some of the key people who would be my new management team. Acting CEO Hakon Østberg had generously invited me to dinner at his home where all of the general managers of the foreign offices of Wilhelmsen Lines (WL) were present. In addition, I had conversations with group CEO Leif Terje Løddesøl, main shareholder Nils Werring, and Wilhelm Wilhelmsen, as well as the three Finnish investors who all sat on the board of WL.

Based on these conversations, I understood there were plenty of challenges. A lot of good internal work had kept the ship on an even keel after the Partnair accident on September 8, 1989. A number of new, capable people had been employed as replacements for those who had perished. Østberg, together with Løddesøl and Hans Christian Bangsmoen, who had been the face of the company after the tragedy, had kept the organization's spirits up with strong, supportive leadership. Understandably, no one had tackled the strategic problems yet. Things had revolved mostly around repairing and consolidating.

Thus, I had not arrived at a wrecked vessel—more like a vessel that had not yet set a new course after weathering several storms. Without clear goals, no one was sure how to proceed. The board had given me some free rein to figure that out. Yet there was a clear requirement that the company would be managed and developed in its market niche—the roll-on/roll-off segment (Ro-Ro).

That was not difficult to understand either from obvious market possibilities or from the shipping line's proud and solid historical traditions since its beginning in Tønsberg in 1861. That was the year Wilhelm Wilhelmsen, the tanning master's 22-year-old son, came home from France with the bark ship *Sophie*. Although his father had owned the ship for some years, this sailing ship was the beginning of Wilhelmsen's Shipping Line business. The bark *Mathilde*, often referred to as Wilhelmsen's first ship, was not purchased before 1865. In addition, the Wilhelmsen family did business with many kinds of private businesses and in partnership with other families.

In the 1880s, Tønsberg was the largest port in Norway and Wilhelmsen was Tønsberg's largest shipping line as well as one of the major companies nationwide operating sailing ships. Many predicted the sailing ship's demise at the time because of the arrival of steamships. Yet in 1886, Wilhelmsen bought its biggest sailing ship ever, the *Enterprise*. Meanwhile, the company was preparing for a new era by purchasing the company's first steamship, the *Talabot*.

Perhaps these two events alone are a picture of Wilhelmsen's fundamental business philosophy, and similar to what I encountered over a hundred years later: stick to what you are good at but keep searching for new opportunities. Despite the fact that the shipping line had ridden many of the same wave crests as the rest of the shipping industry, and had been cast into the industry's deepest wave troughs, its ability to remain afloat has been quite remarkable. The shipping company's specialty was fixed-shipping routes. It would certainly have been bad business had they not persisted in trying new things, such as special ships for automobiles, containers, bulk, oil and gas, supply ships, and drilling rigs in the offshore industry, bringing in capital from new owners and even investing in cooperative businesses and several other areas.

Still, it was rough when oil prices plunged during the winter and spring of 1986, and the company problems were so large that it had to sell ships and rigs, renegotiate its debt, bring in fresh capital from new co-owners, and lay off almost 600 employees in its own companies and partly owned companies. It was a costly lesson from those expansive offshore years in the first half of the 1980s. A sharp fall in oil prices generated the crisis and drove Wilhelmsen and a number of other offshore shipping companies toward the bottom.

In 1988, Løddesøl became group CEO in Wilh. Wilhelmsen. He came from the Norwegian Credit Bank (DnC) and had previously been CEO of Wilh. Wilhemsen from 1974 to 1980. He knew both the shipping line and the shipping industry well, and was an important addition for solving the financial tangle and rebuilding morale in the company after the offshore crisis.

The company was saved after only two rounds of debt negotiations in bankruptcy court.

The shipping line was also suffering, but it was still profitable. It was, therefore, split into a separate company in 1988, Wilhelmsen Lines AS (WL).

The company's ninth ship, which was to be baptized *Topaz* in Hamburg on September 9, 1989, was intended to have a central role in the new shipping company because it would mean that the company could offer an established, daily, round-the-world service. Half of the approximately 100 employees in the shipping company took part in a drawing to attend the naming ceremony. They traveled by charter flight from Oslo Airport on September 8 around 4 p.m., the day before the ceremony.

The rest of the staff was invited to a performance at the National Theatre in Oslo to see the play *Monkey Business*. After the curtain for the first act, theater director Ellen Horn appeared onstage and asked all employees from WL to immediately go to another room, where they learned the plane carrying their colleagues was missing. Based on the information presented, there was little reason to expect anything but the worst possible outcome. All 55 on board had probably perished, including the executive director and the rest of the top management of the company. Løddesøl and Information Director Hans Christian Bangsmoen had traveled ahead on regularly scheduled flights to prepare for the event.

I began about six months later. The newly purchased ship in Hamburg was named *Torrens*. The shining name *Topaz*, chosen by the employees in a naming contest, was never used—and most likely will never be used. From ancient times, there has been a certain superstition in both aviation and shipping regarding challenging the forces of nature. For example, many airlines do not have a seat row number 13. SAS never had one. Only after taking over Braathens did the number 13 get into the SAS cabins.

Wilh. Wilhelmsen ships' names all began with *T* because early in the company's history, ships whose names started with the letter *T* had the greatest fortune at sea. Since nothing had ever caused greater misfortune over the shipping line than the prelude to the baptism of *Topaz*, no one took chances on giving a ship that name again. Such things may seem meaningless when seen from a rational and business perspective, but they are deeply rooted culturally and therefore just as important a consideration as other religious and cultural codes.

I used the first period of my new position to try to find out what kind of organizational culture I was dealing with and soon discovered that it was split in two. The split was between those who had been in the company when the tragedy occurred and those who had come afterward. Many in the former category still struggled with a mixture of grief and guilt. A refrain heard over and over since the night in the theater when they had received the shocking message was how ironic it was that those who had lost the draw had really won—and vice versa.

I was familiar with such reactions. During the deadly fire in the Caledonien Hotel on September 5, 1986, in Kristiansand, several of the 14 deceased had been employees of the SAS Trading Company. I had been with them two days before on an island outside of Kristiansand, where we participated in a fun team exercise. Afterward, we enjoyed a great evening at the hotel. I went home the next day, while the seminar continued with strategy work for one more day.

At 4 a.m., an electrical fault in the hotel's basement ignited a fire that quickly spread to all wings of the 13-story hotel. The smoke was so thick that no one got out via the emergency exits. The reason was structural weaknesses in the building. It must have been hell. The windows were blocked because the handles had been removed. Some people smashed windows and were rescued or jumped out. On the top floors, guests had to be picked up by helicopter because the Kristiansand Fire Department's ladder trucks weren't tall enough. This hotel fire was the second worst in Norway. In addition to the 14 victims, 54 people were hospitalized, many of them SAS employees.

As a leader, there is only one thing to do when this happens: travel as fast as possible to be present for relatives and survivors—just as Løddesøl and Bangsmoen had done, returning to Oslo from Hamburg as soon as they learned about the Partnair tragedy. In such situations, there is not much one can do. The feeling of powerlessness is no less strong than the feelings of sorrow, meaninglessness, and injustice.

Nevertheless, the effect of leaders *not* participating in such things can be even more dramatic: heads of state and other top executives have learned this when they considered the need for presence based on rational—not emotional—points of view. Reason cannot override an erupting volcano of conscious and unconscious emotions that arise when a disaster strikes—whether one person suffers a sudden and unexpected death or many die due to major accidents.

Managers are not always capable of understanding the symbol of their actions, large or small, but if there is one thing that workers at every level notice and talk about, it is what their leader does—or *fails* to do—in certain circumstances.

As a new manager of WL, I, therefore, had the benefit of some experience with the communal mourning process, while not having been personally involved in the mourning process I now led. Thus, it was easier to look at myself and the tragedy from outside, as well as the new employees who had silently begun to wonder how long the "old gang" would be preoccupied with the tragedy. They were eager to move on. "The show must go on" was probably some of the talk in the yard.

There was also turmoil on the side of the owners. The Finnish owners, who had become connected with emergency services after the offshore crash in 1987, wanted the company to go public. The Werring and Wilhelmsen families, who still owned 50 percent of the shares, were against this. They wanted to maintain as much control as possible over the old family dynasty. The establishment of WL was also a reminder of that.

As the new leader, I was hampered very little by ownership disputes. One reason was that both parties agreed that the operation of WL had to be expanded, and there was always a good atmosphere between the parties—even in board meetings. All the owners wanted—as most owners do—was the most value growth. Another reason was that they spent so much time on themselves and each other that they were less involved in the details of the actual operation. I would come to regret that when we purchased the next two ships.

My main goal in the beginning was to obtain an overview. I decided right away not to pay attention to the famous "first 100 days" by which new leaders are reportedly measured. The organizational problems were too deep. Eventually I discovered that there were cultural differences not only between the new and old employees but also between departments and within departments—regardless of the time of employment. In addition, there were not only differences; in some areas, there were also conflicts and direct enmity that went far back in history and also affected new employees.

The most prominent organizational problem, and probably the reason for many of the conflicts, was lack of clear roles and lines of responsibility. Many walked around with the idea that they had responsibility for specific tasks and areas, and they acted accordingly. Suddenly they would find that someone else had encroached on their "territory" or made decisions that blocked or restricted their freedom—without advance communication. Such things did not contribute to good fellowship.

The air disaster most likely contributed to exposing and destabilizing a part of these structures. Some employees lost their allies and worked on enlisting new ones. Others lost their opponents and thus gained somewhat of an advantage. Regardless, "bad chemistry" was the order of the day between several people in key positions, a phenomenon that in my experience has more of an organizational origin than human, and often results from unclear goals, few incentives for interaction, and little corporate culture consciousness. That was expected. After the fierce punishment Wilhelmsen had taken due to the offshore market crash, the new organization had not had time to stabilize before a new disaster hit them.

At SAS, which was somewhat sheltered, it had been difficult to establish crisis understanding, and thus the need for change, even after two years of deficits. However, employees at WL were much more receptive to something being done within the organization. Nevertheless, I noticed some fear when I hinted, in advance, of possible changes. Fortunately, only a handful seemed to experience that as a direct threat.

Such is life. I don't think I ever implemented a change process where everyone immediately jumped on board. In fact, quite the opposite. The normal change support distribution is: 25 percent for, 25 percent against, and 50 percent on the sidelines until they see which way the wind blows.

There can be many reasons for that. Some do not see the need for change—they think things are good enough as they are. Some perceive it as criticism of earlier efforts and results, and a personal attack on their pride. Others wait out the situation to see if the process works, or they are afraid of the extra work. Some know they have privileges that are not productive and are afraid to lose them. The latter will often work actively against the process and often end up finding something else to do when they realize that the battle is lost.

At SAS, we called those layers of change opponents the Rockwool-layer. At Wilhelmsen, there was a less flattering maritime name: Grease Barrier, something that repels everything, no matter how hard one tries to establish the need for changes.

In my experience, the greatest gain comes from working with the neutral 50 percent—those susceptible to influence. If you can accumulate up to 60-70 percent support for new goals and methods, and establish binding systems for leadership, maintenance, development, and rewards that send homogeneous signals through the organization, the new corporate culture will do the rest of the job. Either people are on the team or they go elsewhere.

To increase the precision of my observations, I decided to do the same as I had done with good results at SAS: a climate analysis. Through Scandinavian Leadership, we developed some simple statements that all would evaluate on a scale from 1 to 6. The statements were

1. I know what importance my job and tasks have in order to reach the company's goals.

2. I consider continuous learning as an important part of my job.

3. I am proud to work at Wilhelmsen Lines.

4. I find that departments at the main office work well together.

5. In my department, I am encouraged to find a good balance between work and leisure time.

6. It is easy to solve problems that arise between departments in the headquarters.

7. In my department, we know which segment of our work makes up the final delivery to our customers.

8. I feel that senior management cares about what is happening "on the floor" in the company.

9. I feel that there is good information flow between the top management and my department.

10. In my experience, people in my department mostly speak positively about management.

11. I am involved in the work to make annual action plans for my department.

12. I participate in the decision-making process for issues that are important in my department.

Based on these statements, we knew we could get a precise picture of how people perceived the situation both in the company and in their part of the organization. At the same time, we would be able to ascertain a great deal about what kind of leadership style was practiced in the various departments and thus the real responsibility each employee had.

When we were about to start the survey, more fear became apparent. Many were hesitant to answer the questions, just as they had been at SAS Cargo. They believed that the answers might be used against them. Things loosened up only after we promised full anonymity and that only the consultant company would see the answers. We also made it mandatory that everyone participate in the survey if he or she wished to continue to be employed at WL.

The results of the study were not surprising. As with many businesses at the time, employees were used to having most decisions made at the highest possible level and for those decisions coming down as orders in the organization. In addition, people felt there was poor interaction between departments and poor conflict resolution. On the positive side, the vast majority were proud to work at Wilhelmsen and felt their job had importance. I was reminded of conditions at SAS before the turnaround.

I noticed the same tendency in management meetings I held each day in the beginning, as was company custom. They called them morning meetings, and that was what they were. Cases that could have been decided one or two stages further down in the organization were presented here. This was a taxing situation for me who, for a decade, had practiced the principle that it is better to ask for forgiveness than permission.

In actual discussions, I also noticed that there was a large gap. The managers openly sent different signals out to the organization; historically, this is the main cause of poor interaction. Meeting discipline left a lot to be desired. People continuously arrived late. There was always something important they "just had to do," which in practice wasted everyone's time. I easily solved that issue by locking the meeting room door at the stroke of nine, and then we handled the absentees' cases. After a couple of such meetings, everyone arrived on time.

The management group spent most of the time on issues related to day-to-day operations instead of planning ahead. Many were not even qualified to understand the plethora of details, so there was practically no room for strategic and fundamental discussions. It was obvious that they were used to being given overall guiding principles, rather than developing them based on knowledge and experience found throughout the company.

Such is life in autocratic organizations where leaders are accustomed to giving orders and making decisions instead of allowing the ones who do the work to figure out the ideas and how to implement them. Dissemination occurs via *information*, which is a one-way process, rather than *communication*, which is a two-way process, derived from the Latin word *communicare*, which also means "to do something together" or "to bind together."

In such a system, the leaders often receive little feedback and correctives from the most important parts of the business: the ones in closest contact with customers. Thus, it is business as usual—corresponding vulnerability to changes in the market and framework conditions. I recognized much of the production-oriented organization that SAS had been.

Good ideas rarely come from the top leader. They come through the organization and often have their origins in the operational part of the business—that is, from those who have the most contact with customers and other connections. Good managers succeed in bringing these ideas out. To do that, there must be a culture where employees feel that they are on the team. That feeling comes when they get the necessary freedom to think innovatively and receive corresponding responsibility to introduce new methods with the authority to implement them. That requires a great amount of openness and seamless communication, and assumes that all employees know their place and their tasks in the organization.

Financial and other administrative systems also were not adapted to this way of thinking or working. They were not management tools but reactive systems that registered revenue and expenses, and how much time went to different tasks. There was no ongoing assessment of the inputs that gave the best results in value. Everything was based on hunches. At the time, of course, few IT systems had come much further than word processing and accounting. Nevertheless, it was not state of the art that was lacking but mind-set.

Some departments ran well with customer focus and goal management; unfortunately, they were the exception.

People in most departments worked using their own judgment, and some ran terribly. One of the latter was the Department for Ship Management, which, in an attempt to have more to do, took over part of the actual ship operation from one of our international partners, Barber International, of which Wilhelmsen Group was sole owner. It turned out that the department lacked sufficient professional skills to perform the operations at the same level that Barber had. Meanwhile, relations with Barber, upon whom we were still dependent for this, had soured.

This was what some of the controversy on the owners' side was all about. The Finnish shareholders wanted most of the ships' technical management placed in the WL organization in order to make the company completely independent, probably so they could get it on the stock market to maximize profitability. One of the Finnish owners had even allied himself with the leader of the WL Ship Management Department to try to strengthen this. Wilhelmsen regarded taking advantage of Barber International's expertise as more natural.

The situation came to a head when the poor business climate developed into direct conflicts between Wilhelmsen Lines and Barber International in a number of areas. These were eventually resolved when I met with the management of Barber and we drew up a battle plan for how we would move most of the critical tasks associated with ship management back to Barber.

This conflict-ridden relationship probably contributed to my first major mistake at WL after less than six months in the executive chair. It turned out to be not one but two mistakes and would cost us dearly, but at least it was a valuable lesson. If as a leader you do not have the required expertise for decisions you are about to make, you'd better ensure that you have an organization that is so secure and open that you have full access to the skills you lack.

In this case, both were lacking. First, I knew a lot about planes but only a little about ships. Second, there seemed to be little tradition in Wilhelmsen for communicating bad news all the way to the top of the organization. Instead, a "please the bosses with what you think they want to hear" culture ruled, which again resulted from many people who worked on *positioning* themselves rather than on *qualifying* for positions. That is how poor climate and communication get started, and results in poor decision-making for senior management.

The twofold mistake was the purchase of two Con-Ro ships (combined Ro-Ro and container ship) that received the names *Tarn* and *Tarkwa*. Internal experts from our ship management department inspected the ships in the usual manner. According to the report that eventually reached us in management and the board, they evaluated the ships as good. The assessment was that they needed relatively small tweaks to adapt them to our use. The price was also reasonable. Thus, the management group recommended to the board that we buy the ships.

Just after delivery, the engine room exploded on *Tarn* and the ship drifted helplessly around the Mediterranean with neither engine power nor control. A short time later, the same thing happened with *Tarkwa* in the southern Atlantic Ocean. Worse, both ships were already commissioned for service in our trade between West/South Africa and the United States.

As it turned out, both ships had so-called Pielstick engines, which were widely known at the time as being well suited for short-haul ferries and other vessels that had a lot of berthing time in port. They took little space on board but required extreme attention during operation. Consequently, they were not well adapted for long voyages where the engines run for days—sometimes for several weeks—at a stretch.

Based on their specifications, the machines could have been in good condition. For that matter, they could have also been properly maintained by the crew under the previous owners, even during longer trips. It amazes me to this day that not even members of our very competent board asked critical questions about the purchase of these two ships. However, the board actually did its job when basing the decision on what seemed a thorough investigation, and where even I, as the company's top administrative leader, didn't have the qualifications to ask the right questions.

In hindsight, I can hardly hang the responsibility for this on anyone other than myself, especially after I found out that several of the most experienced people at Barber International had disagreed with the purchase of the two ships. They knew that there was a reason why old Pielstick ships always had three engines: one was always out of service. However, as long as the conflict between Barber and Wilhelmsen lasted, Barber remained silent.

That mistake spurred me to make changes in the company's culture and in the relationship with our most important partners. I saw how vulnerable the company and I were without in-depth knowledge in an autocratic system. It would probably take longer for me to gain the necessary knowledge on my own than to access the expertise already existing at all levels of the organization and with our subcontractors.

The first thing I did was abolish the meaningless daily morning meetings, replacing them with weekly management meetings and significantly raising the threshold for cases. That meant many decisions got pushed down in the organization. Initially, that was interpreted by some as meaning "the pilot" they had put into the driver's seat for the company did not have the guts to make decisions, not wanting to put his stamp of approval on decisions they really should make. In that way, he avoided responsibility, they felt, which was wrong. A top manager is always 100 percent responsible for any act committed in the business—no matter how impossible it was. As a leader, you can delegate responsibility, decision making, and tasks but never free yourself from your overall responsibility for what happens on the team.

Occasionally, I made mistakes in employing people for leadership positions, both when it came to professional competence and ability as team players. As someone new in the company, I probably trusted recommendations and references more than my own gut feeling. I did not yet know the management group well enough to be able to assess how a new person would fit in. Someone might work excellently in one setting but be totally unsuitable in another. It is unfortunate for both parties if the latter is not discovered in time.

Eventually I became familiar with the outside organizations, including the largest in Australia, Japan, and the United States. There, I encountered much of the same as during my first time in leadership at SAS USA. There was a lot of tea and coffee drinking, lunches and dinners with wine and dry martinis, and other representations that were certainly nice enough, but which produced little or no results for the company. We cleaned this up without creating too much dissatisfaction within the organization.

I constantly questioned what they did and why they did it this way or the other. We began to work more strategically in considering all activities and budget entries to determine what served the company's and customers' interests, just as we had during the most result-rich efficiency rounds at SAS.

During that time, we began to look around for possible business partners, even among shipping companies and other companies that were our competitors. We discovered, for example, that Nissan Motor Car Carriers regularly sailed cargo ships with Japanese cars to Europe but made the return trip empty. When we contacted them to see if it was possible to charter the ships for the return trip, we found that Wilhelmsen had already entered into such an agreement in 1975. That agreement seemed to have sunk into oblivion after the Partnair accident, where much unshared expertise and history had disappeared, making it difficult for new managers to carry on.

We renegotiated the agreement to charter ships on the way back to Japan and used them to transport cars from Europe to Australia. In this way, we not only maintained but also strengthened our position in the Australian market without having to make additional investments. The agreement was also very good business both for Nissan's shipping company and WL.

We operated several lines, which were actually worldwide services between Europe and Australia/New Zealand, through South Africa or the United States. Shipping lines are based on fixed routes between the same ports, in contrast to tramp lines where the ships go everywhere with different clients and products. New lines are established when there is basis for permanent traffic, such as establishment of a new factory or new open markets. Typical products of shipping lines include automobiles and other vehicles, agricultural machinery, construction equipment, mining equipment, rail cars and locomotives, paper, and other heavy loads that are part of fixed logistics.

The company climate analysis had revealed turbulence and conflicts in many places in the organization. I had the same impression after making the rounds, holding meetings with everyone, and speaking with individual people at all levels. I also saw that the lack of interaction in top management had filtered down. This was particularly evident when trying to implement projects where collaboration between several departments was one of the critical success factors. Even daily routines were not set up to facilitate interaction. For example, many managers ate lunch by themselves instead of sitting with their coworkers.

Despite various organizational challenges—or perhaps for that very reason—I saw a clearer picture of the enormous potential we had in an ever-expanding market, particularly in Ro-Ro shipping. On one occasion, with many employees present, I said that there was no reason that WL could not be the world's largest Ro-Ro shipping line in the next 10 years.

For many of the employees, this was the first optimistic speech they had heard since before the offshore oil collapse and the plane crash. It was only much later that I heard others had said that the talk was proof that "the pilot should have stayed in the air." It took 12 and not 10 years to build Wilh. Wilhelmsen into the world's largest Ro-Ro shipping company. I think it is interesting to note that our focus was not on being the biggest but rather on continuous improvement and being the best.

After the rounds of climate analyses, we developed a coaching program with Scandinavian Leadership for all managers of WL. The program began at the top, where everyone in the management group, including me, would evaluate each other and ourselves in relation to the three areas at which we thought we were good and three areas in which we felt we should improve ourselves.

This was obviously threatening to some and revealed underlying agendas in others, which led to a few adjustments in the top management group. Some managers think they are equally good at everything. My experience is that all managers have good and less good sides, which results in their making good and less good decisions when they are on their own. This is the point of defining and accepting the consequences of the management group as a team, where we can complement one another and make more good decisions than bad ones.

In the beginning, people might feel insecure about exposing qualities which neither they nor others are particularly satisfied with. In addition, when they experience that unclear roles and indistinct areas of responsibility create vague expectations, this further strengthens their insecurities—especially for those who have been more concerned with their *positions* than their *functions*.

Insecure people have an extra challenge because they face their own vulnerability through such processes. Some choose to pull back rather than to continue in the process. Others try to work against it, making subversive alliances other places in the organization. It becomes an unacceptable situation if they persist after everyone has agreed on the path and solutions. If the management team doesn't send consistent signals to the rest of the organization, they will never be sufficiently effective.

A management team that is not in sync undermines an organization's teamwork as much as when a trainer, a team leader, and a devoted football dad stand on the sidelines all shouting advice to players on the field on how they should tackle various situations. In the first place, it destroys the players' possibilities for finding their own solutions. In the second place, the players become confused because they don't know whose advice to follow.

Those who have the necessary inner motivation to do the best possible job—not primarily to adorn themselves with pretentious titles—eventually feel strengthened by the recognition that leadership is not a solo game but a game of teamwork. Then they experience airing out and discussing both their strong and weak qualities as an added security. Eventually it becomes a part of the daily routine to decide who would be the best to solve different tasks and what development areas the individual needs to work on to become better. In this way, a learning organization is established, which in my experience achieves much more and performs better than one with people who feel they have already reached the top in abilities and results. Things only go downhill from such a position.

After requesting that a couple of management team members find other jobs, I felt we had established the required honesty and transparency in the whole team. Only then could we begin to promote the program further in the organization. That happened through what we called *climate seminars* that we arranged with groups of 30-40 employees for two days at a remotely located hotel.

Everyone in the top management group was present at all the seminars and participated actively in the program, which was very simple. First, we underwent the climate survey, which highlighted the need for changes. In the beginning, we did not place too much emphasis on the differences between the departments. Climate research is a development tool and not a success-rating contest.

Nevertheless, as we eventually began to investigate the relationship between climate and results, we found that there was a large correlation between climate development and results development. We instituted the Blowtorch Prize that we handed out with great pomp and circumstance to the leader who had managed to turn his department around with the best financial results. This went hand in hand with doing culture changes within the department.

As working tools, climate surveys show the way forward and contribute to development of the organization. At Wilhelmsen, the most important development areas were the same as in most other businesses I have come across: a holistic way of thinking, interaction, and customer orientation.

After presenting the results of the surveys and reflecting on them, people worked in groups to come up with measures that could stimulate development in the three areas mentioned above. It turned out that they were closely connected. When we began to focus on customers and the purpose of the company—and not individual positions or departments—the goals presented themselves clearly. We immediately saw the necessity and advantage of interacting in order to reach the goals.

In addition, both managers and coworkers cooperated in developing some leadership principles that everyone would keep. Leadership principles benefit both managers and employees alike in the organization. No one is better in evaluating a leader than his or her employees. That was, in reality, what we had accomplished with the climate analysis.

Of course, some would say that good leader principles are always simple. That is exactly why the process of developing them and converting those principles into a practical tool for everyday life is so essential. Otherwise, they quickly become no more than a piece of paper in a desk drawer or a file on the computer along with all other good resolutions.

Leadership principles, rules—or whatever they are called now—are brought to life by the leader. They must be on the agenda in all meetings, projects, coworker conversations, employment interviews, reward systems and planning, and evaluation of good and bad projects. Only then will the words, which appear to be truisms, have real substance and meaning. They become part of the corporate culture—yes, they *will be* corporate culture.

We picked out four leading principles with some sub-points specifying what they meant in the daily workplace:

Honesty and transparency. Not only when convenient, but also when inconvenient. Admit mistakes so that others can learn from them. We don't do politics.

Open information. (With politics, we meant fighting for their own interests.)

Loyalty. To the company and to our employees. Not going with the flow, but always expressing their opinions. When the decision is made, step up to the plate even if you were against it. Do not send conflicting signals. Not servility—not "please the boss."

Delegation. Be dependent on coworkers. Work toward a coworker's success. Guide and help the ones to whom you have delegated responsibility. A delegation of responsibility is not a disclaimer. Delegation means the balance between authority and responsibility.

Responsibility. Everyone must take initiative and act within his/her own area of responsibility. Have an overall view—work for the company's total result and not suboptimization, which is in conflict with the total score. Support your colleagues in the group. Responsibility and expectation should be defined for each employee.

All development areas and measures were placed into a system of action plans and followed up each day as part of general reporting at meetings and gatherings at all levels. We also had a handful of coaches from Scandinavian Leadership who followed up with each individual in his or her daily work.

Coaching always started with the individual's personality, proficiency, and development potential. The goal of coaching should never be to treat everyone the same but to develop everyone individually and understand how each can perform best for the benefit of the whole company.

We used external coaches and each other (peer coaching) to develop ourselves as leaders. During the peer coaching, we sat in pairs and discussed what we could do for each other that would make us a better management team. The rest of the management team sat and listened. The principle was that everyone would talk with everyone else. That way, we became an incredibly close-knit group. No one was perfect; we learned to trust one another. Thus, we had no need to dissemble when we got involved in discussions or demanding decisions.

We continued with all employee meetings, climate studies, and coaching. After a year, the new organization began to solidify with a shared image of where we stood and where we wanted to go. Only then—when we could see that the new corporate culture began to exist—could we begin heavier strategy work. Creating a strategy is not really an art form: implementation is the challenge. To do it you must first work on the culture. I once heard an expression: "Culture eats strategy for breakfast." That is what corporate culture is really about: an experience I have had through all the change processes of which I have been fortunate enough to be a part.

Now when I look back at the first leadership principles we developed at WL, I might have removed some of the *nots* and replaced them with their positive counterparts—that is, what we *should* do. The way the situation was at the time at Wilhelmsen, I still think it was right to stress some of the un-culture that existed in the company.

When an organization starts to get into step, it is natural to remove negative mind-sets, in the same way a doctor changes a patient's medication when they begin to get well. Leadership principles must be dynamic and subject to regular revision. They then remain more alive than principles "passed once and for all." They make us think and reflect, both over the results and ultimately over the conditions for creating them.

So it was at WL, as the organization grew and adapted to new waters. When, after thorough strategic evaluations and a dramatic tug-of-war, we finally got the Norwegian America Line (NAL) on the team in November 1995, it was time for a new—and even more thorough—process.

12

GROWTH AND VALUES

WL had barely begun a strategic process when almost its entire leadership disappeared into the North Sea. Understandably that process stalled. The discussions in the boardroom between Wilhelmsen and the Finnish owners produced no clear course for the company. The large deviations within the organization did provide fertile ground for clear priorities. WL was, in reality, a ship that largely sailed where the wind took it—though with a fair wind.

For the company did earn money. That was probably one reason the board had not addressed the strategy process. As long as it was possible to conduct business as usual with good margins, it was easy to delay working on strategy. One might argue that the board discussion on the initial public offering was strategic in nature, but it was primarily an owner strategy—not about where the company would earn its main income in the long term and how it should organize business to get the best possible results.

Parallel to the climate analyses, we initiated mapping of strategic areas in which we needed to do something. Some of those areas were purely internal, such as financial management, systems development, internal control, results, and organizational and personal development. Other areas included both internal and external conditions, such as market and customer orientation, representation abroad through our own offices and/or agents, as well as ship operations and maintenance. The biggest external challenge was the question of where the main market lay. Was it in container shipping or Ro-Ro? Was it a combination of both, where the company mostly operated? Besides—how much of our customers' logistics was it possible to gain in order to raise our value chain?

The internal strategy areas were integrated as a natural part and consequence of the process of climate analyses and coaching programs. Many of the practical solutions were conceived in seminars at the remote hotel and refined in follow-up discussions in what had now become a host of new venues for interaction. It was easy for the majority to realize that if we were to bring the organization in line, we also had to have systems in place that reinforced this.

Measures for increased market and customer orientation were also established due to these processes, just as they had been at SAS when responsibility for operations was moved out as far as possible in the organization. Discussions naturally progressed to how we would be represented abroad, and what was the most appropriate way to operate the ships.

WL had some of its field offices abroad, but at the same time used a network of agents to market and sell services for a large number of shipping companies. We realized this was not optimal. It was difficult for the agents to have closer contact with clients to promote our interests, which, in turn, prevented us from having closer contact with them. The agents represented more vendors, and they had to balance concern for their principals with their own profitability. For us to develop the cooperation to include more than just traditional shipping at sea, we would probably have to establish more of our own field offices.

When it came to the operation of the ships—or *ship management* as we call it in the trade—we arrived at the opposite conclusion. WL had tried to take over more of this with bad results. Now, when we systematically looked at what challenges this entailed and what it would cost, we saw that we would have an uphill climb to be as competent as our sister company, Barber International.

The most important acknowledgment made through the strategy process, which stretched out over the first three years and would have major implications for how WL eventually evolved, was that we were too small in the markets in which we operated to be able to influence rates and framework conditions. We were at the mercy of the major competitors in both container shipping and Ro-Ro ships. Also, we didn't have the muscle to position ourselves where we could care for more of the customers' total logistics operations. The so-called 4PL—fourth party logistics—had been a business area for larger logistics companies, such as UPS, Federal Express, and others.

The conclusion of these evaluations was that WL had to grow. Growth can take place in two ways: either organically, building stone on top of stone, or by acquisition. It looked as if the biggest growth opportunities would be in the market for Ro-Ro ships, especially automobile transport. Admittedly, both major Japanese and European auto manufacturers had begun to build up their own production units in their main import countries, but it did not seem so extensive that it would significantly curb the increasing automobile transport between the continents.

Then, when we evaluated our acquisition opportunities, the answer became obvious. Large competitors handled container traffic and we would hardly have the financial strength to purchase them. There were several opportunities within Ro-Ro. One of them was the Norwegian America Line (NAL) that was equal in size to us and also had weathered unrest and major movements on the owner's side at the end of the 1980s.

Wilhelmsen had previously collaborated with NAL through Norwegian Specialized Auto Carriers (NOSAC), which was a type of pool for auto transport. However, the 1986 economic crisis at Wilhelmsen had forced the company to sell most of its 20 percent of NAL to another shipping company, which also ran into problems and sold the shares to others.

Wilhelmsen had 1 percent of the remaining shares in NAL at the beginning of 1995 when we decided to try to gain control of the company. Wilhelmsen purchased a number of smaller holdings and gained up to 37 percent, but that was the end of it. As it happened, Norway's largest tanker shipping company, Bergesen d.y., decided that it needed a new and more stable foundation to stand on, in addition to oil and gas transport. This situation would develop into a real thriller. Via the brokerage firm Fonds-finans, Bergesen managed to get its hands on enough shares that it unexpectedly controlled 42 percent of NAL.

The NAL board recommended that Wilhelmsen have control. The board already saw large synergy effects of combining much of the shipping line with Ro-Ro ships between the two shipping companies. However, Bergesen did not yield. Fondsfinans now played more than a bro-kerage role. It purchased a shareholding just big enough to tip the scales between the two companies. By the be-ginning of October, Bergesen, Fondsfinans, and other sup-porters had a bare majority share in NAL of 50.17 percent.

CEO Løddesøl had experienced many antics from brokerage firms during the wild era which led to the late 1980s banking crisis, and which had turned the DnC he headed at the time upside down. This maneuver from Fondsfinans was more than he could accept. The other-wise sober-minded CEO exploded and raked the two owners of the brokerage firm over the coals.

In Wilh. Wilhelmsen's 150th anniversary book, the incident is described as "a WW takeover attempt delay-ing tactic," which led also to upset foreign investors. The book mentions, "There was considerable reason to ask questions both concerning Fund Finance's integrity in this blocking move, and the Oslo Stock Exchange's role in a game that was obvious to financial market players."

Although Bergesen had, on paper, won the tug-of-war, Løddesøl did not consider the battle lost. He wrote a more composed personal letter to Morten Bergesen (the major shareholder of the Bergesen Group) and discussed the different parties' interests in NAL and which solutions would best address these interests, including a fair representation on the board.

One month later Bergesen called Løddesøl and said Wilhelmsen could purchase the shares of NAL—provided the price was right. The mighty tank ship billionaire had not had an attack of a guilty conscience—he had cast his eyes on another shipping company also for sale, one that was more in line with Bergesen's principal business.

In any case, there were no concessions—or chess moves—when Bergesen showed up at the negotiating table with one of the two agents who had caused Løddesøl's outburst. However, since the CEO was normally more rational than emotional, negotiations went smoothly, although Wilhelmsen now had to fork over 13 crowns per share.

On November 17, 1995, Wilhelmsen owned 92 percent of the shares. By the end of the year, we owned NAL. That doubled the size of the company I was to lead. It was, therefore, time for a new process to merge two cultures into one.

Some might be tempted to look at an acquisition as an opportunity to guide the purchased company into the fold of the purchasing company. Fortunately, I had been through so many restructuring processes that we did not fall into that trap. Even though NAL as a company had been tossed between many different owners for almost 10 years, there was a lot of culture and pride in its halls. Many of the NAL employees had hoped they would end up with Bergesen as a long-term and stable owner. With that in mind, we could not just inform them that Wilhelmsen's rules and values would apply from now on.

Culture construction is tricky enough in one company. Merging two cultures can be even more demanding. You must do it as if building an organization from scratch—the more blank pages, the better. Still, you cannot avoid the fact that many will focus more on differences than they will on similarities. Everything you can do to balance the organizations' positions will help in the process. Even though this involved an acquisition, it was important to look at the actual integration process as a merger.

It may take considerably longer to break down old bad habits and reluctance than to give people the freedom of new ideas. In our situation, there were more basic assumptions, which gave fewer reasons to stick with old ideas. The companies were about the same size and operated in much the same areas. In addition, the timing of the acquisition coincided with Wilhelmsen moving its main office from Oslo to the new premises just outside Oslo in July 1995, where the still-existing NAL company also moved in January 1996.

What we did first was take a step back and then start with the idea of merging the companies. The purpose of this was to give everyone a balanced view of why it was a good idea. The companies were in a similar market situation but sailed on different seas. Even more important, the emerging collaboration between us while stock acquisitions evolved had produced good business results.

We established a management team using three executives from each company, thus reflecting the companies' equality. When we defined the roles and responsibilities of the individuals in the management group, we emphasized expertise, not history. Basically, we reset all positions and discussed who was best suited to each position.

The process was much the same as I had been through at SAS and in the first management group at Wilhelmsen. We considered each other and ourselves as to areas where we were proficient, where we needed to develop ourselves, and in which functions we would most benefit the new company. Even though most were already familiar with each other, we were thorough. Ultimately, I ended up as CEO and NAL CEO Nils P. Dyvik as deputy CEO and chief financial officer. The rest of the management team members fell into place on their own accord.

The next step was building an organization that was best adapted to what had now become common customers and markets. We defined the operating organization and various support functions according to that pattern. A number of changes of roles and responsibilities, and certain redundancies in some areas, resulted. We resolved this with offers of early retirement, relocation, or retraining. Some managers were hired by the cooperative company United European Car Carriers, which operated short-haul automobile freight in Europe.

Thanks to having spent so much time in the initial part of the process where everyone had the opportunity to form the same picture of how things were—and how things needed to be—all readjustments were rather painless for both managers and employees. In companies where layoffs and restructuring are thrust upon the employees, the entire operation is often paralyzed by disappointment, guilt, and sorrow—much as with major accidents. As a result, things get worse and more cuts have to take place.

In six months, the new organization began to take shape. Then we were able to start with climate analyses to fine-tune the integration. A number of the questions were different than they were in the first survey we conducted in 1990 since this was a new situation. This time, however, there were no discussions as to whether or not people would participate.

Most important was finding out if we had succeeded in placing responsibility and decision-making authority far enough out in the organization, and if the leaders of each of the departments and units actively contributed to stimulating this. As always, it was a development opportunity for all of us who were leaders. Therefore, we also started with new coaching programs and a collective value process.

We had worked more with these types of processes at Wilhelmsen than at NAL. Four leading principles, used actively both internally and externally, had developed into values for the entire company and become four enduring key words that would characterize all of our activities:

- honesty
- loyalty
- cooperation
- responsibility

Now when we started a process for our new organization, we discovered that these values were still sustainable. The primary reason was that we kept them alive and related them to our daily work. When values are attached to recognizable and practical situations in everyday life, it is easier to create processes that everyone accepts as his or her own.

Values don't decorate a company; they are the organization's human compass, reminding everyone how to solve tasks in order to reach goals. Those values characterize all decisions, work methods, actions, and results where employees continually ask questions as to whether what they have done, what they do, or what they intend to do is in line with the company's values.

- Have we been completely open and honest?
- Is this action loyal to our business strategy?
- Have I involved all necessary parties in this decision?
- Are we exercising proper responsibility in relation to our level?

We actively used these values in every possible situation. I did not hold a single meeting or presentation—internally or externally—without stressing the four values in one context or another. Sometimes I grew tired of hearing them back as an echo of my own voice, but I knew that if I didn't keep them alive as top leader, they would soon begin to fade and eventually die. Then the whole process would be in vain. Revitalizing dead values has nowhere near the same effect as maintaining strong ones, if you even manage to bring them back to life at all—something which we later had to do.

Precisely because the values seem so obvious, it is important to maintain them. You can compare them to your health. As long as you are young and vigorous, you don't give health a second thought. Unless you have a congenital disorder or contracted one early in life, you take health for granted. When you begin to have poor health, you start to see the need for care. At that point it might be tougher—and sometimes not possible—to get into shape.

All managers—and especially top management—have to lead by example. I found that one of the most important things I could do was look for and point out examples of where the values worked. I did this by encouraging everyone to celebrate milestones and commend associates who achieved results—and relate both as much as possible to the four value concepts. All organizations need and are fond of role models and heroes. The trick is in revealing that they are the company's values and that we created them.

It may sometimes be appropriate to maintain a hidden threat to highlight the consequences for not following the rules, but there is considerably more incentive to using good history and elevating heroes, rather than by punishing those who have made mistakes. In businesses that have traditions of rewarding their employees, the withdrawal of a reward may be a strong enough correction, especially when it is properly justified and presented in the form of questions:

- Why did you make this or that decision?
- Why did you choose this or that solution?
- What might be the reason that your results last month were not as good as they normally are?

We conducted employee discussions twice a year where individual relationships to the company's values was one of the central themes. It turned out—almost without exception—that the ones who had ingrained these values in their minds and acted in line with them were also at the top in producing results. We saw the same patterns in the annual climate analysis: the departments that scored the highest on value awareness delivered the best results.

We already earned good money, which both the board and managers might have settled for, feeling we had reached as far as a shipping company could reach. Now it was only to grab hold of the top—and stay there. Fortunately, none of us felt that was especially tempting. Instead, we began to look for opportunities to jump the curve.

We knew we still had to focus more on our clientele. Even though we reduced the number of agents and concentrated more on our own field offices, including NAL's offices which supplemented our own in several places, we were still far down in the customers' value chain. We were the shipping company that transported customers' goods at sea, while much of the rest of the money-making logistics occurred over land.

Even where we were able to cover a large geographic area, such as in Germany where we had taken over the entire agent system, we felt that we did not have sufficient customer contact. Actually, we had the same problem we had when using agents: no matter how hard we tried, we could not reach the decision-making level at the customer businesses. Therefore, we did not climb any higher in the value chain to develop customers' total logistics.

Other companies were taking more and more of that position. Pure logistics companies, such as UPS and Federal Express, and land-based transport companies, such as DB Schenker and others, not only earned money from transport assignments, but also—and more importantly—took care of all logistics for their customers.

We felt that we were in a better position to be able to do this; we already accounted for the heavier part of the freight for many of the customers, especially within the auto, agricultural machinery, and construction machine industry. Therefore, we decided that we wanted that position. But how would we attain it?

The answer came naturally. First, we needed to talk with clients and find out what their needs were. Then we had to make sure that we had the necessary skills to be able to deliver what the customers needed.

The biggest limitations for getting to the appropriate level with the customers were in our own organization: "We have not done this before," "We have not tried this before," "We don't believe in this." In addition, we made another blunder. We expected that the customer was at the top of the team, but we did not send the top of our own team. The Germans, in particular, are preoccupied with hierarchy. The same is true in the Far East. As soon as we signaled that people from our own top management would meet with customers at a similar level, the meeting appointments were set.

It was revealed in these meetings that several of the larger customers believed that the transport chain out to their customers could be much more effective. Thus, the doors were, in effect, open with one of the most prestigious customers: Mercedes in Australia. Now all we had to do was show that we could come up with good options and holistic solutions—and above all, that we could deliver.

In the meantime, we had researched where we could find the best expertise on logistics. We made a deal with Cranfield University in England, where they had a department and a profiled professor of logistics. He had not only outstanding expertise in the area, but connected us with several companies where logistics posed one of their biggest challenges, including the major British department store Laura Ashley. As it turned out, logistics was a separate subject area where both our customers and we faced an enormous learning curve.

We used the professor and his large network of contacts for all they were worth, as lecturers, motivators, and advisors. The more we learned, the more clearly we saw how crucial logistics was for profitability. In some areas, especially when handling large volumes, it spells the difference between success and failure.

Meanwhile we found that climbing up the customer's value chain on the transport page was not rocket science. It was simply solving more of the customer's challenges: not just shipping freight, which we were already good at, but the whole journey—from door to door; essentially, the same principle we had tried with business passengers at SAS during the mid-1980s. We would still experience that it took time to learn the logic of logistics. We made several mistakes, both with our own coworkers and with contractors.

The first attempt at the door-to-door concept at Wilhelmsen was unfortunate. This time it was not because we forgot an important relationship, as we had with travel agencies at SAS, but because we failed with an important hiring. The customer it affected was not just anyone: Mercedes in Australia, one of the first we had access to at a high level.

We agreed that we would take over the whole logistics solution for exports to Australia. It was a complex operation with plenty of details, partly because the cars had to be modified for the Australian market. Thus, we were talking about shipping not just the cars but also auto parts—and wth very tight deadlines. We thought we had a watertight plan but discovered too late that we could not deliver according to the agreement. The reason was the human factor: the person responsible for the agreement retired soon after, and the one we hired to take over was not qualified to follow up. Mercedes was not amused.

Our skilled Australia Managing Director Peter Dexter did what he could to try to correct the wretched business and at least explain why things had gone awry. But the reason we had failed to deliver was of no interest to the German car giant. The agreement ended.

We had, of course, included field offices in the value processes. Nevertheless, there was no concealing the fact that it was more challenging to keep them in the fold, not only because of cultural differences. Other issues always arise between field offices and the main office than between home offices and the main office.

The highest authority always goes down through the line on the home front. In the relationship between headquarters and field offices, anyone from the main office is viewed as an authority—regardless of his or her level. In effect, this means that everyone coming from the main office, by his or her actions, helps set the standard for how people in the field office view how things should be—regardless of how he or she represents the company's values.

I have no basis to say if that was what happened in this case. But I experienced a number of times at Wilhelmsen and SAS that feedback came from leadership at field offices, sometimes directly and sometimes indirectly, where it was questioned as to whether there were changes in the company's priorities when it came to strategy, business, and ordinary behavior. Unfortunately, there are people in all organizations who believe they are free from domestic bonds and obligations the minute they get on a plane or a boat bound for another location on the globe.

Fortunately, the bumpy start with Mercedes had no ripple effect. Later both Volvo and BMW in Australia became customers. And eventually Mercedes came back to us. The mistakes we made were so obvious and in such violation of what we had defined as best practices that we were able to learn from them. The main lesson was that logistics' responsibility requires an extreme level of precision. Each link in the chain is equally important. It reminded me of the fight for punctuality at SAS. The challenge at Wilhelmsen was that not everyone was used to thinking that way. A ship—especially one in a shipping line—would, of course, arrive on time. But after several days on the open sea, navigating canals such as the Suez and Panama as well as other obstacles in the politicized and risky waters, a little slack was still accepted.

In addition, others had responsibility for land transport. That meant that the shipping line was at the mercy of the elements not only on the high seas and political complications by land, but also on others' ability to deliver on either end of the transport. Our customers saw this as an area in which there was considerable potential for increased efficiency if one company had the responsibility for the entire transport.

For us, this also meant efficiency gains. For example, our Ro-Ro ships went all the way up to Hamburg, Germany, both expensive and not very profitable because we had to sail slowly on a long river. Transporting the cars by speed train from Hamburg to ports such as Antwerp, Belgium, and Bremerhaven, Germany, significantly cut total transport and sailing time. Thus, the ships could make several trips between destinations and earn more from investment and operating expenses.

With agents and external logistics companies taken out of the chain, it was easy to make a case for a win-win situation for our customers and for us. There is no shame in telling customers that you earn money on what you do for them; quite the opposite. It guarantees that you are actually interested in doing a good job for them.

We were thus in the process of getting close to more of our customers, as we had wanted. This created more challenges than just delivering more services with a higher level of precision. If we were to keep and develop the role of strategic partner in the field of logistics, we needed to cultivate the customer as well as ourselves. Thus, it was time for a new process where we could figure out how we could do that. Eventually we arrived at four key points:

1. Anticipate the customer's next move.
2. Be in the forefront of the customer.

3. Find a way to the customer's perception of reality.
4. Use Custom Relation Systems (CRS).

The next step was to find out what this meant in practicality for each department, and whether each department had the right attitude and skills to be able to play such a significant role in the client's life. I felt that this decisive step took us in the right direction. This was customer orientation in practice—and the true consequence of jumping the curve. Then we fell into a new trap.

Satisfied as we were over the results of obtaining our own market and sales machine in the most important places we operated, we felt we should have our own logistics apparatus as well. So we began building terminals, depots, and storage on land. That did not go as well. Fortunately, we discovered quickly that it was outside our area of expertise and that we should instead purchase these services. The lesson was that it is also possible to go too far in jumping the curve.

Along with this, we realized another thing we had not taken full account of: we were accustomed to being way down the value chain as a subcontractor to various logistics companies and agents. Now we were suddenly in the driver's seat with our customers and had to deliver a range of services we did not have the expertise to produce ourselves. We soon found out that we were also not qualified to buy those services.

To be a good purchaser, you need the same skills and knowledge as the vendor. Many businesses put off production of a variety of goods and services, and simultaneously dispose of so much of their own expertise that they no longer have the ability or capacity to follow up and assure the quality of their deliveries. This means that they become totally at the mercy of the vendor. We see this especially in IT, where many companies have no inkling of what type of systems they have purchased.

Many also foolishly outsource operation of the switchboard, canteen, security services, and other functions—without even realizing that these functions make up the most important part of the customer front for many businesses, both internally and externally. This was reminiscent of the first cost-cutting rounds at SAS with costs cut everywhere, with no thought about areas that had potential for being profitable or which were important to customers and employees.

It can be expensive to carry out development in all areas—very expensive. However, outsourcing vital functions without being able to control the deliverables in line with the company's values and customer perspective is even more risky. The more important a site is strategically, the more important it is to assure its quality. Many leaders, for example, view the canteen as a necessary expense and try to run it as cheaply as possible. I would say that a well-run canteen that has a proper host function is very important to job satisfaction—and a hygiene factor that can contribute greatly to employee motivation.

Some leaders also believe they can get rid of responsibility by outsourcing parts of the business. That is as basic a misconception as believing that responsibility is no longer yours when you have turned over project implementation to a coworker. If you select a security company to operate reception and security, it is still corporate's responsibility to ensure that that company maintains security at the required standard. Security companies only do what they are told, unless they have an agreement with extended powers. It was the management at Mercedes who had to answer for the disgruntled Australian customers and business partners when we could not manage the first demanding logistics deliveries for them.

WL owned 12 ships before the merger with NAL. With NAL, the fleet more than doubled. The important work of integrating tonnage to ensure that we capitalized on our capacity continued in parallel with internal processes and the development of cooperation with our customers. We renegotiated many customer agreements and merged several field offices.

By now, collaboration with Barber International functioned very well and improved once we strengthened competence in our own procurement organization. I daresay that we eventually brought the best out of each other, as good relationships always do when roles, responsibilities, and expectations are clarified. This applies to all interpersonal relationships where communication is simple and clear because all have the same understanding of what they want to achieve.

We often confuse our message with too much information that the recipient is unable to deal with. When people feel that they are ill informed, it is just as often because there is too much information as when there is not enough. When I traveled and spoke publicly to employees and customers, I sometimes used an example of how the amount of information is inversely proportional to the importance of the message: the "Lord's Prayer" consists of 54 words. The base text of the US Constitution is 300 words. The European Union directive for the import of caramels at the time contained 22,000 words.

The more one says, the greater the chance for misunderstanding. With today's fast-moving media, it has become easy to inundate us with news and messages—without any thought about what is essential and what is excessive. Viewed this way, perhaps Twitter's 140-character limit can seem disciplining, except to those who have more on their minds and text several messages in succession. So basically, the status quo—especially if they have not thought through what they want to say in the first place and eventually discover that they even disagree with themselves.

13
A SUCCESSFUL MARRIAGE PROPOSAL

Australia was one of the biggest markets for WL. After we lost the Mercedes contract, we hired people with the right skills. We also built up respectable logistics on land and became by far the biggest player in the field of auto transport. But there was one auto manufacturer we didn't have: German BMW, which was big in Australia. They had a large contract with the Swedish Wallenius Shipping Company that transported their cars all over the world. But for some reason Wallenius was reluctant to sail directly to Australia. Instead, they carried the cars to Japan where they were transferred to a Japanese shipping company that transported them to Australia and New Zealand.

BMW worked on getting Wallenius to open a direct line to Australia, but this still didn't suit the Swedes. Thus, we obtained the contract when it was up for renewal. That apparently hit Wallenius hard. Perhaps they feared we would take over more of the freight for BMW. In any case, they decided to sail directly to Australia and got the contract back.

It was an expensive commitment. Wallenius had to build their entire logistics from scratch and soon realized that it would not pay off. So they came to us and asked if they could purchase space on our ships and in our land-based operations. That was the start of a very beneficial collaboration. Eventually, we saw other opportunities where renting capacity from each other was beneficial rather than sending half-empty ships to the same ports and even full ships one way and empty ones back, as Nissan had done. We also discovered that our main lines were more complementary than competing.

One day in late 1998, Christer Olsson, CEO of Wallenius Lines, and I held a confidential meeting at a hotel in Port Douglas, Australia, to discuss how we could further develop this cooperation. We were each strong in our own areas and in each shipping line in the parts of the world we operated. Together we controlled about 18 percent of the worldwide Ro-Ro market.

We soon circled around the question: could we merge the companies into one? We soon concluded that we would have gains in almost all areas if we merged instead of operating on our own, especially when it came to utilization of capacity and leveraging our largest customers.

After airing our opinions with our respective boards and owners, we received the go-ahead to proceed with the more detailed assessments. We chose three people from each company in addition to ourselves. They would calculate and consider all aspects of a possible merger. The results looked good. The relative strength of the two companies was about the same as it had been between Wilhelmsen and NAL. A joint company would have 80 ships.

We drafted a merger agreement just after the 1999 New Year. In contrast to the public acquisition of NAL, this agreement was kept strictly secret within the small circle of owners, board of directors, and group of trusted employees working directly on the merger. Because our mother company, Wilh. Wilhelmsen ASA, was listed publicly, the competition authorities to whom we wished to present the possibility for merger before it was publicized to others, including our competitors, could add additional terms for a decision. Still, we had a strategy if word got out. We created a clear-cut, thorough communication program to meet information needs internally and externally for all possible situations. The presentation was continually adjusted as disclosure of information and negotiations progressed, so we always had ready answers if there was a leak.

After everything was formally in place, we sat down to determine responsibilities in the merged organization. Fortunately, the discussion about leadership roles was as pragmatic as it had been for the NAL merger. We agreed that I probably had the best qualifications to manage the integration process between the two companies. Thus, I was once again the CEO. Christer Olsson was effective in representing the company externally and had a good relationship with the owners. He would be an excellent chairman of the board. And that's how it was.

Just before we announced the merger agreement, we presented it to our respective global management teams. I attended when Christer Olsson gathered the entire management team from Wallenius Lines at Stockholm Airport–Arlanda and he said: "Meet the new boss."

There was dead silence. No one said a word for what I felt was a long while, even though it may have actually lasted only a few seconds. History of Norwegian-Swedish industrial cooperation was bad. Only 20 years before, the infamous Volvo agreement had gone down the drain when Norway purchased 40 percent of the Swedish auto manufacturer in return for Sweden getting sections of the oil reserves on the Norwegian continental shelf as corresponding value. The activities on the shelf were successful, but the Swedish auto manufacturer encountered challenges and the deal fell through. This was still foremost in the minds of our brothers in the east. At the same time, talks between Telia and Telenor during 1999–2000 were in a critical phase and were scrapped soon after. And now we were presenting a completely negotiated Norwegian-Swedish merger where huge assets on both sides were affected. Everyone knew that the only thing that had functioned as a somewhat equivalent Scandinavian cooperation was the old SAS agreement from 1946.

But no one threw tomatoes at me or used profanity: people in top management in the business world are more polite than that. Eventually, I think most people saw the rationale and the potential, even if at the time they might not have seen how it would play out in practice.

I spent a good deal of time explaining the merger, and I think I even managed to communicate that the integration process began with both companies as equals. We would conduct ourselves neither nationalistically nor politically, but professionally. When the meeting was over, I felt the atmosphere was pretty good. It seemed that even those who had expressed the most skepticism began to believe in the new reality.

The environment was already positive in my own management team. While Wallenius had been around for a number of years, we had fresh experience from a very successful merger process. Any uncertainty and skepticism during the merger of Wilhelmsen and NAL had long since disappeared due to our success in developing the long road to a homogeneous corporate culture based on our common values.

We discussed how we should develop—or should we jump the curve—while we were still on the rise. When you have reached the height, it is often too late, just as the sun inevitably goes down after passing its zenith. People and organizations develop more energy on the way up and on the way toward the goal than when things level out or suddenly begin to decline. For me, the old saying still holds true: "During the ascent, everything goes well," unless it is so steep that you don't get off the ground.

Strategic management is not only about finding new opportunities and defining new goals but also exploiting the organization's energy at the appropriate time. A new merger might be a mistake if the organization has not stabilized itself after the previous one. When people feel they are being tossed here and there, they are more likely to stick to their own perceptions of how things should be and are less susceptible to new impulses.

Organizations that rest on their laurels after reaching their goal hardly notice when others pass them, and suddenly, relatively speaking, they are relegated to a lower position. Then it is much more demanding to rally the troops and climb up again. Suddenly the goal is no longer to be the best but to survive. That limits freedom of action and greatly affects the mental attitude and belief in what you do.

Due to the thorough preparation and preliminary work we had done, we were quite confident that the merger would go our way. The scopes we presented to the competition authorities in our respective countries and in the EU showed that we would not dominate and there would still be healthy competition in the Ro-Ro market. We showed that a merger would make shipping more cost efficient and, therefore, more profitable for our customers. These advance meetings were very important.

One of our competitors, Høegh, was smaller than both Wallenius and WL had been separately. They would hardly be thrilled with an even larger competitor. Before we made the merger public, we informed them and our other competitors and important relationships.

It has been my experience that you make more progress when you are transparent than by going behind the backs of people or deliberately surprising them, even though parts of the process must necessarily take place behind closed doors. The news came as a bit of a shock to them, and I know that especially Høegh worked quite intensely afterward in the EU and with other authorities to try to stop the merger.

When I went to Japan just after we released the news, I was greeted by a large delegation from our biggest Japanese competitor. At first they were suspicious of the merger, and I was pumped for information about what we wanted to accomplish by it. Fortunately, I could be completely open about the background for the merger starting with the cooperation in Australia and the fact that the two companies were complementary and not overlapping.

The way our Ro-Ro lines existed before the merger, there was little real competition as long as we delivered what the customers demanded. We literally sailed in our own parts of the globe.

At this point, I was both CEO for WL and deputy group CEO in Wilhelmsen Holding. The history behind this was that we had actively worked to integrate most of Wilhelmsen's different activities in the world. After the merger with Wallenius, we felt that I had to resign as deputy group CEO in the holding company because I would now serve two equal owners. It was inappropriate to have a central leadership position at one of them.

The owners retained ownership of the ships. The new Wallenius Wilhelmsen Lines (WWL) formally chartered ships from the Norwegian and Swedish company. All operations and earnings would be in the new company, which was formed into one company, commercially, operationally, and culturally. The amalgamation was a considerably bigger job than the integration with NAL.

One reason was the cultural differences between Norway and Sweden, which in some areas is considerably larger than one would think. The Swedes are more like the Germans. They are more autocratic, centrally governed, and have greater respect for authority. Although they may appear quite jovial and be on a first-name basis, in reality they are more formal, have a strong belief in the system, and are methodical. Norwegians are more egalitarian and make quicker decisions—often as much based on intuition as from long and systematic studies. The exception to the rule is large parts of public administration. Norwegians in general have considerably lower respect for authority. Courtesy is next, while the Swedes hold on to formalities even in informal settings.

In addition, we had a cultural mix in all the field offices and on board ships. In order to be successful in establishing a common corporate culture, we first needed to crack common cultural codes and customize processes according to those, in the same way as with building individual development processes of a person's mentality and assumptions.

The location of headquarters was an early subject of discussion. Ideally, there should have been one main office in one place. At the very least, the commercial and operational functions should have been together. That was not possible for internal political reasons. Therefore, we needed to find compromise solutions, something I've never been a fan of. But that's not because I am not amicable or like to modify requirements when necessary, for example when customers or employees find themselves in difficult situations. When compromises are based on position and convenience resulting in less-than-perfect solutions, I get a hollow feeling—the opposite of satisfaction.

With two equal partners from two different nations and with strong owners on both ends of the keel, it was inevitable that central functions had to be allocated. Initially, the commercial departments, with the exception of the communications department, were located in Oslo; that department and management of the European offices were located in Stockholm. The operational department was also located in Stockholm, while the technical operating department was divided so that the Wallenius ships were operated from Sweden and the Wilhelmsen ships from Norway.

Because that became cumbersome, all commercial and operational activities were moved to Oslo. The Swedes were not pleased, and I would never win a popularity contest in the old Wallenius berth. That didn't bother me—a manager doesn't need to be popular, but he does need to maintain sufficient respect and confidence to be able to make and carry out decisions that are best for everyone.

We also tried to move the European office from Stockholm to Antwerp, but opposition was so great that both popularity and confidence tumbled. So we abandoned that plan and concentrated on getting the best possible structure in the field offices, which at the time of the merger were doubled in several areas of the world and consisted of a number of agents who had collaborated with Wallenius.

We agreed to discontinue all agent agreements and concentrate on our own offices. In some places that meant expanding Wallenius offices; in other places, Wilhelmsen had a more ideal location. What we could never agree on was whether to locate the office where the customers were or where the ports were located. In the end, it was the individual office's strength and competence that determined the location.

In most places the molding and merging process went well, but in Japan it was rough. Both ship owners had large offices there. Several managers didn't want to relinquish their positions. I spent a week constantly on the move there. We negotiated during the day, went out to eat and drink in the evening, and then repeated everything the next day with new formal processes. The endless topic was clarifying roles and responsibilities. That had to take place in such a way that no one lost face. The social dimension in Japan is important. You have to give people the feeling that they are in a winning situation, even if they are placed somewhere else on the chart. Eventually we put a new organization in place that everyone could live with. When we moved both offices from Yokohama to our new premises in Tokyo, it became easier to concentrate on the new organization, rather than to mull over how things had been before.

In the United States, we agreed on the Wallenius office since it was the strongest. Nevertheless, the manager of one office began to dismiss a number of talented employees because he perceived the merger as an acquisition and not as an equal merger where the most competent from both companies were kept on board. I had not been informed of this. I finally discovered it during a general meeting when people complained. Fortunately, we managed to salvage some of the best people when we clarified the situation.

I experienced management of the field offices as some of the most demanding in both SAS and Wilhelmsen, not just because of cultural differences and susceptibility to inaccurate signals from the head office, as I had previously seen. The field offices represented the most important part of a company that had the whole world as a market. Consequently, they had to be managed in line with the company's goals and values but not overridden; otherwise, responsibility, creativity, and drive would be crushed.

I don't think I ever found a formula for maintaining the proper balance between the main office and the field offices. But I experienced two significant factors. One was that the skill in the field and at home had to be at the same level in order to achieve the right balance and avoid an imbalance of power and its corresponding danger of quashing creativity and energy.

The second factor was a close follow-up from management's side with questions that required responses consistent with how things actually are and not how one would like them to be. If you ask, "Are you all right?" or "How's it going?" everyone will answer "Yes" or "Good."

If you ask about results that have been achieved since the last time, how they are achieved, and what the goals are for the next period, you get considerably closer to the truth.

In addition, if you are specific but open and neutral in the follow-up questions, and politely request documentation, you get a close semblance of reality. Openness and neutrality are important. No one likes to divulge bad results, especially in the Far East—that impacts honor, and people will go to great lengths to warp reality.

At the same time, when you are in the field, it is important to exhaust every opportunity to preach values and desired working methods. Even if I got tired of hearing my own message, I experienced how necessary it was to remind people of the organization's responsibility to protect and develop corporate culture in line with what the common guiding principles were for the new company, WWL. As always, I got more information when I asked open questions and greater assurance that those I met were on the right path when they felt they had found the appropriate solutions.

We humans are really best at two things: what we have come up with and what we think we have come up with. The latter is the most important result of good coaching. The trick is asking people leading questions formulated so that the people themselves give the correct answers. Anyone can learn coaching. Therefore, we put everyone with management responsibilities through courses and training programs on a regular basis. In fact, this was more about technique than talent, even though as with all talents, some had it more naturally than others.

We also made use of the measuring tools we had, such as climate analyses, 360-degree feedback, key performance indicators, and other reporting systems that uncovered actual conditions and not desired ones. Overall, this helped to reduce the distance between the main and field offices, and to decrease the number of surprises. I must admit that we didn't have full control of everything and everyone at any time. In any case, there were fewer mercantile Mayday messages to deal with.

We didn't always hit the bull's-eye at headquarters either. We made a couple of bad hires and now and then sent the wrong people to customers and field offices. This brings me back to the starting point for this book. Leadership does not consist of a set of absolutes where you know whether this or that method always provides optimal results. Perhaps that is precisely what makes leadership so exciting: you must always customize your methods to your goals and to the people with whom you wish to achieve those goals.

As I now proceed toward the end of this mission of discovery, trying to see patterns in my own leadership, I see that I used some methods where more good than bad results were consistently achieved. I can already see the contours, but there still are a few processes that remain, which I believe can alter perspectives somewhat.

14

BUT WHAT DO THE CUSTOMERS SAY?

WWL now had close to 4,000 employees on land and just as many on board ships. I felt we were well under way with the managers, but all the employees had to go through a process where we established a common picture of our goals, values, and methods. The processes were easier on the ships where the command structure was clear: the captain's word is law. It has to be this way when managing a risky business which, in principle, a large ship is. However, the captain's leadership is only as good as that which he develops together with his crew. That was precisely why it was important that our shipping managers had the company's values and working methods ingrained as well. Just a few months later, we would experience the importance of this when one of our large ships ended up in a very delicate situation.

Wallenius Lines was a well-run family shipping company with roots back to 1934, when Olof Wallenius started the business transporting vegetable oils on the ship *Soya*. In the beginning, the *Soya* and several other ships sailed charter routes but eventually began to specialize in Wallenius Ro-Ro and auto-carrier ships. The development of the shipping line gained momentum in the 1960s with container shipping after the formation of

Atlantic Container Lines (ACL) along with American interests carrying Ro-Ro and containers.

Wallenius Lines evolved to become Sweden's largest shipping company and was often called "The Opera Line" because Olof Wallenius, an opera enthusiast, named all their ships after famous operas. When he died suddenly in 1970, the shipping company remained in the family. In 1989, Wallenius pulled out of ACL and the container market to concentrate solely on Ro-Ro and car carriers, just as Wilhelmsen did.

With the merger, many pointed out that it must have been difficult to agree on the color of the ships. Wallenius ships were green, Wilhelmsen's ships were red. The main shareholders of Wallenius suggested that they might be green on one side and red on the other, something that would be a gimmick for navigation at sea.

It ended with us continuing to operate both green and red ships but with the name WALLENIUS WILHELMSEN painted with large white letters on the ship's hull. However, increasingly more ships were "green" inside with our commitment to environmentally friendly measures, including engines that ran on lower sulfur fuel. It cost more but produced fewer harmful emissions—far below international requirements. This exemplified our values mind-set. A shipping company of our size, which strived to run a clean business in all areas, was also morally obligated to operate as environmentally clean as possible. This especially had been a trend in Wallenius for many years. We realized that, in the long term, this would also result in maximum profitability. Customers became more and more committed to these values. We experienced that it was good to operate an eco-friendly business.

Wallenius Lines had not run any of the value processes we had implemented at Wilhelmsen Lines. The somewhat autocratic management style I encountered at Wilhelmsen Lines a decade earlier was still the norm at Wallenius Lines. As with Wilhelmsen Lines, Wallenius Lines had produced good results, but it, too, was unsuccessful reaching a high-enough level in the value chain to be involved in developing the customer's overall logistics.

Of course, it would have been tempting to try to force Wilhelmsen Lines' values on Wallenius Lines' employees, but we knew that would not work. Values are something the individual must acknowledge, so they become an inherent part of a person's conscience, operating and steering their thoughts and feelings in the right direction. At Wilhelmsen Lines, we had had a more conscious relationship to our values. But after completing the climate analysis in the completely new company, we saw that Wilhelmsen Lines' dominated departments also had needed to bind those values tighter to the customer perspective.

Values were certainly on people's minds but not yet embedded enough to drive the daily work throughout the organization. It was time to take those values one step further and strengthen them as business stimuli. This was actually a good discovery, for it meant that the new value process we started would apply to all managers and employees in the entire new company.

Once again, we started with the top management team, but this time the process took an unexpected direction for many. Through the Center for Creative Leadership, I had come in contact with a former priest and now organizational psychologist from Scotland, Dr. Brian Hall. He had developed the concept of Values Technology. This encompasses the psychological monitoring tool Q125, which is also used for recruiting. It can also be used as an evaluation tool because it reveals not only the person's personality traits but where they are located on the value scale, as well as what priorities they have with relation to this. In short, the aggregation of all scores gives a clear picture of where the organization is on its value scale. With this tool, Hall brought us deeper into the world of values and what they really mean to a business as well as the individual person.

This was uncharted territory for many of us. We had been accustomed to understanding and experiencing values more as ethical guidelines to help us choose between right and wrong. Through this work, values became the foundation of the company and individual manager's and employee's development. They were not only the guide for managers' speeches at the Christmas table, but for everything we undertook in our daily work.

Fortunately, we set aside a whole week for the process with the entire global management team. We didn't understand all the implications in the beginning. Many were impatient and annoyed, and justifiably asked: Are we going to sit here and waste a week of our time relating to issues and dimensions that are not even close to what we do on a daily basis? We are leading a newly merged shipping company with 80 ships and 8,000 employees, and we have to sit and drag out subjects that are as distant from our ships and waters as we could possibly get.

We had a plan for that. Hall understood that as results-oriented and impatient managers, we had limited capability to direct a real value process because we thought we had the answers already or we wanted the results even before we really started the process. Instead, they now led us—or attempted to lead us—into completely open waters where the intent was to help us understand the deeper differences between theory and practice. As top executives, we needed to get into our inner dimension and ingrain it under our skin so we actually felt a bit different when we left.

We were nowhere near fully trained, but we understood a few new, critical perspectives when it came to values. What does it mean if I am on one side of the scale or other in relation to the company's values? Where do I stand when compared with the different values? What does my own perception of values mean for those I lead? And what can I do to keep my own limitations from becoming limitations for others?

The tool was as easy and as complicated as a value process must be for it to yield results and cause a ripple effect on all major and minor business tasks. It clearly indicated that value development was not a quick fix. Essentially, it was an ongoing process in which the implementation phase was the most demanding: that is, binding our values to the customers' and operations' tasks. The maintenance phase was still the most important. Values must be repeated and taught in everything we do: planning, implementation, evaluation, and continued development.

In his special way, the old priest managed to establish the understanding of this so deeply in the entire top management team that we came out of the process with a completely different mind-set of humility with relation to customers. Throughout the previous years' logistics operations, we thought we knew customer needs quite well. But did we? Although we knew a lot about what they needed, were they really satisfied with what we delivered? How did they view us as business partners? Did our values correspond with what customers expected of us? We knew considerably less about that.

We had thought that as long as they purchased our services, they were satisfied. After a week with Hall, we understood how risky such an evaluation was. What did we know about all the little annoyances that might have built up at lower levels and that, in total, could contribute to disrupting the entire customer relationship? In addition, what did we know about what we *did not* deliver but that customers still wanted, without their having managed to convey the need to us clearly?

The start of the value process at WWL had led us not only to a deeper understanding of what values were but to a deeper understanding of our customers. We understood that we were still too far from our customers to get the optimum out of our collaboration. We were not on a sufficiently high level to find the real answers to what they expected of us and how they evaluated us. It was one of the main acknowledgments I had made since my studies in Nuremberg when I discovered that no matter what challenges I face, it all depends on me and my ability to find solutions.

I believe that this recognition of the customer perspective was the reason that the rest of the process was so successful. The value development furnished a meaning that most people understood. This was important because our jobs were based on our customers. For that reason, most were receptive to the rest of the process. We also experienced that it was easier to make a case to the inevitable naysayers. It was considerably more difficult for them to oppose the customer dimension than if it had only been an internal process.

Values and leadership principles are the foundation for the culture that most want. The trick was in developing processes and systems, and to make them so binding that the degree of compliance had consequences either in the form of positive or negative measures. When we brought our value processes closer and closer to the customers, the results that those values created became increasingly visible.

Before we moved forward with the internal process, we conducted a round of in-depth interviews with all our major customers, which in practice were several of the largest global producers of auto, construction, and agricultural machinery, mining equipment, rail cars and locomotives, gas turbines, and other global energy industry equipment. In addition, we created a written survey that was sent to our smaller customers. The purpose of these was to get the most nuanced answers to three basic questions:

1. How do you feel about WWL as a company?
2. What are we good at? What can we do better?
3. What are your expectations of us as a supplier and business partner?

We used an external company, supplemented by our own people, to create and carry out the surveys in order to add adequate professionalism to the interviews. The answers were consistent in both surveys. The key findings were, perhaps, not totally unexpected after the process we went through with Hall.

1. We thought we were better than what the customers thought we were.

    a. We thought we had clear objectives on what we should focus on and thought we delivered in line with those objectives.

    b. Nevertheless, there were a number of specific areas where we were not good enough. As is commonly known, the devil is in the details; viewed together, the details make up the whole, and that contributes to forming the final impression of our delivery capability.

2. Customers had greater expectations than what we thought.

    a. They expected us to think more proactively about them and how we could develop their logistics services and ours even better. In practice, they expected us to sell more and deliver more.

    b. They also expected that we would serve them with the same professional standards and level of service—no matter where they met us, regardless of whether the contract was negotiated and entered into at headquarters. This point dovetails with 1b above.

3. In addition, the auto industry, especially, expected us to work actively on the environmental side and to publicly document that we were in the forefront of development in this area.

All managers and middle managers were put through Q125. Using the results of these assessments and customer surveys as the basis for seminars, we arrived at five new basic values determined by customers' concerns and where we felt we had the most important development needs.

1. Customer Centered

All decisions and actions shall be based on how much we can possibly do for the customer. It is important to create a clear, common picture of the customer in our own organization.

2. Empowerment

All employees must feel they have sufficient freedom
and responsibility to make decisions that immediately provide answers to questions and resolve issues
for the customers—without having to go through
their supervisor. This is also important for internal
processes.

3. Learning/Innovation

We must be able to provide customer access to solutions and expertise, which are at the forefront of what
we all assume are customer needs. We shall contribute to a new way of thinking by the customer and
work on continuous improvement. We shall think
on behalf of the customer and contribute to the customer's improvement. (We had a lot to do in terms
of customer expectations, both in terms of further
logistics development services and staying ahead of
environmental requirements.)

4. Teaming/Innovation

In a global company, working on cultural understanding and learning what to do and not do in
different countries is important. We need to work
smarter by creating teams that can take advantage of
the synergy in the decision-making skills and professional and cultural expertise at the operational level.
(We were not very good at this either. We lacked
multicultural understanding and, consequently,

started courses on this to make it easier to collaborate—no matter what kind of nationality or mentality
we encountered.)

5. **Stewardship**
    We have a responsibility to the community and the
    outside world. Our role is to act as a host or host-
    ess—one who caters to the customers and the compa-
    ny's interests in relation to this.

    How shall we take care of our people and con-
    tribute to their development? How shall we take care
    of our investments in the form of ships and shore
    installations? What are we doing on the environment
    side? (Some of the basic ethical values from Wilhelm-
    sen and the environmental awareness of Wallenius
    came into their own here. It was not difficult to get
    general support that this also included honesty, loy-
    alty, and responsibility.)

Later in 1999 and 2000, we ran value processes in all parts
of the organization with the goal of creating awareness of
why and how the values can guide everyday life for the
benefit of all parties. We worked simply and practically, and invited discussions that were as open as possible
about what values could mean for everyone:

- What do they mean for our customers?
- What do they mean for our company?
- What do these values mean for me?

- What do they require of me?
- What do they mean for our department or unit?
- What do they require of us?

All value measures were connected to all individual departments' action plans and policy documents. Eventually, we used the values for managers' and employees' personal development plans, and they became a natural and important part of employee discussions and employment interviews.

This would be a relatively simple process in a small or medium-sized business. With 4,000 employees on land spread around the world on all continents, it was a big project. Based on the clear signals we received from our customers, we never doubted that it was one of the most important investments we made to achieve more satisfied customers and better profitability.

We also experienced that several of our most important customers requested our values. As they now were designed, they contributed toward a feeling that the customers were well cared for. We also received feedback that we were more proactive and the quality of deliverables increased more evenly around the world. We achieved this through regular meetings with customers where we harmonized requirements and expectations based on our customers' and our own values. We were also successful with meeting the customers at much higher levels in their organizations.

To promote further cooperation with customers and suppliers, we created a so-called Performance Improvement Plan (PIP). The more you invite a customer to collaborate, the closer the relationship becomes—and the more it will take to lose the customer.

The danger in making such an elevated list is that you increase the height of the fall. That is why creating good systems binding both managers and employees is integral to lasting success. That was what we didn't do in the first turnaround at SAS at the beginning of the 1980s.

On board our ships, it was up to the officers to establish the correct standard and customize implementation to the existing command lines and routines on board. Most of the tonnage was Ro-Ro ships. The last Con-Ro ship (container on deck and Ro-Ro below deck) delivered was the *Taronga* in 1996. Otherwise, we concentrated on our Ro-Ro market. In 2000, we decided to phase out the container market as customer agreements expired. We were far too small to have influence on prices, service, and capacity utilization. We were at the mercy of the larger players. Bigger is best in the container market.

15
LOGISTICS' LOT

The value process did not vaccinate us against blunders or accidents. Through the merger with Wallenius we received a separate logistics company based in England. It operated all over Europe and was big in Germany where it had a separate subsidiary.

It turned out that this was a truck company with limited expertise in the kind of logistics that we needed. Eventually the company collapsed except for the subsidiary in Germany. It was led by a highly skilled person, who we had thought represented the skill set of the entire company. He did not.

We discovered that we had backed the wrong horse. This mistake revealed that our own expertise as logistics services purchaser was still in a critical stage. We owned a logistics company in the United States that had the appropriate expertise owing to complex operations for the US military. But we had failed to use their expertise and transfer it to the international part of the organization.

Through cooperation with Cranfield University, learning from Laura Ashley, and studies by a number of other companies that were good at logistics, we acknowledged that we still had a long way to go. At the same time, we saw that the auto market was changing. Customers wanted more frequent and faster deliveries in accordance with the "just in time" principle—that is, more efficient logistics.

The major logistics companies positioned themselves for this development. UPS began collaboration with Ford for the distribution of vehicles in the United States. Their ambition was to do the same in Europe, but the auto market there was far more complex and the objective was difficult to implement. We saw this could point to a trend where logistics companies took the position we wanted, taking responsibility for the entire transport chain from factory to retailer. If this continued—without any improvement in logistics on our part—our destiny would be as a subcontractor to logistics companies instead of taking care of the entire chain.

Despite all the knowledge we thought we gained from Cranfield University and others who generously shared their knowledge, we did not yet appreciate that logistics was about building systems to manage the entire transport chain—regardless of the means of transport or where you are in the chain.

Logistics operations include much more than shipping. They include waxing cars to protect paint during transport and then de-waxing before they are delivered. They include maintaining an apparatus capable of repairing and painting damage sustained during shipping, installing additional equipment, and customizing the cars according to local requirements. They also include having storage capacity in different areas between land and sea transport, and a host of other small and large operations.

If there is an area where the devil really does live in the details, it is in logistics. If you make a mistake in a single area, it immediately extends to successive links in the chain. With customers' increasing demands for speed and punctuality in deliveries, the margins for error are correspondingly reduced. In return, we saw that a well-run chain of logistics operations could really make the difference in customers' delivery power and profitability. Thus, we could price our services accordingly, as we had with salmon deliveries at SAS in the 1980s. I learned once again that the closer you can get to customers, the greater the opportunities you have to create win-win situations.

After these acknowledgments, we chiseled out two main courses of action:

1. Our basic foundation (core business) is Ro-Ro sea transport.

2. We shall deliver the rest of the logistics by putting together a professional chain of self-produced and purchased supplies.

We hired people all over the world who were experts in logistics. They not only defined what services we could offer to customers and who could deliver them but also quality-ensured vendors. Soon we saw that we had to run some of the same processes with them that we had done internally in the company, including the PIP process. Since those processes were based on customers' expectations, and which attitudes, actions, and systems vendors needed to develop in order to satisfy them, they were also well suited to our vendors.

We finally felt that we had cracked the code for logistics. It produced immediate results: we got one vendor after the other under our own value-based customer umbrella. One result was that *they* also made more money when we searched for revenue and expenditures together, including via mutual LEAN programs, which we also implemented. Satisfied suppliers are a prerequisite in getting more satisfied customers. In many situations, they are the ones who make up the face of the customer. You need to hunt not only for the lowest price but also for what creates the best value for all parties.

I often wonder how many abandon the merchandise to links they have no control over, whether dealers or vendors. Through the processes we ran, we experienced the ability to control the deliverables in a completely different way. To ensure even quality, we held regular meetings where we evaluated the collaboration. In these meetings, we had full disclosure about quality, economy, results, technical operating questions, and how we felt the collaboration worked. We almost always discovered new development areas, as often happens when both learning and development are part of one system and inherent in the business, and not just something that happens in critical situations or in the company's annual kick-off or strategy meeting.

Of course, good cooperation between us affected our customers. They experienced getting more of what they had requested, not to mention a much more even standard—no matter where in the world they contacted us. Results were also affected: the number of complaints and claims decreased, while turnover and profitability increased.

Nevertheless, there were still "underwater" hazards. I don't think it is possible to have full control of all decisions and details whether there are 4, 40, 400, or 4,000 employees. If you are going to give people responsibility, you also have to accept the fact that they will make mistakes. You achieve nothing if you don't take risks. Willi Railo, a famous Norwegian sports psychologist and business consultant, said that you have to be willing to fail in order to achieve success. I have always said it's better to ask for forgiveness than to ask for permission—as long as it is not based on the same mistake every time.

However, I believe the expression "You learn *more* from mistakes than you do from doing things right" is a myth. A dog that is trained to smell drugs, bombs, or other special things is presented with a wheel containing six containers spinning around on a tripod. One container contains the scent it needs to find; the others contain five arbitrary substances. Every time the dog stops the correct container, it gets a prize. If the dog learned more from failure, it would get a beating every time it stopped one of the other containers but would never learn the scent for which it was looking.

Learning by trial and error can be a rather inefficient and costly way of learning, but it is important to find out what people need to add to their best practices in order to avoid making the same mistake again. A repetition of the error will appear as a *deviation*, which in turn leads to the discovery that the best practices are not ingrained at all. In other words, there is a need for further improvement and learning.

Although we decided that we were going to purchase all logistics services from subcontractors, we suddenly became the owners of the French logistics company CAT, which was owned by the car manufacturer Renault. We made that decision based on the fact that it would ensure Renault as a customer and we would get a well-managed logistics company as well. It turned out to be a particularly bad business venture. The company was poorly run and, in reality, earned no money based on Renault's terms. They were not especially good at logistics either, but in land transport. We fell into the same trap as with the British transport company that went bankrupt. It took a lot of management capacity and a long time to finally restructure the company and then negotiate conditions that gave usable profitability.

The acquisition of Nissan's logistics company in the United States was considerably more successful. It was a solely logistics company that had exactly the competence we needed. Moreover, the conditions in the Nissan agreement were of a completely different character than the deal with Renault. We learned from our mistakes with the Renault agreement. With Nissan, we established a foundation for profitable operations and excellent opportunities for further development of Nissan's potential.

There was still some room for appropriate acquisitions. You must never have a strategy that is so entrenched that it prevents pragmatic solutions and new opportunities. A strategy is not a blueprint but a basis for assessing correct decisions. If you have the answers already, you are probably too late. Either others have grabbed the chance before you and acquired the rewards you should have had, or time has already passed by for the solution.

Our logistics investments were a tremendous success. We started everything from scratch. Today this business within Wallenius Wilhelmsen Logistics has annual revenues of more than 1.1 billion USD and operates at a margin of close to 10 percent of revenue.

Some cultures are extremely good at this, especially within some of the US military departments with which I have been fortunate enough to get quite close due to my position as chairman of the board of the Center for Creative Leadership. One would think, for example, the US Navy SEALs, who are among the world's toughest, are primarily concerned with operations. As it turns out, they have based their technical skills in the field of values and attitudes that any human institution would envy.

Experience shows that the prerequisite for being able to carry out the SEALs' demanding operations is putting the individual person in the center. They then build a system of interaction and a management team around that person, which is extremely responsive to both good and bad signals. With the help of large amounts of commendation and clear feedback, the SEAL Team bonds into units where people learn to rely as much on each other as themselves and where they are so drilled that they do the right things even under very high stress.

I experienced the same on board the US aircraft carrier *Carl Vinson*, which was itself an entire community of 6,000 people. The most prominent was how tight the daily contact was between the high and low ranks, while at the same time there was never any doubt about roles and responsibilities. The safer both managers and employees feel in their roles, the more relaxed they can be in social and practical circumstances. The short distance between leaders and employees also contributed to optimal information flow.

When no one has any interest in coloring the facts to their own advantage, the command lines are very simple—both ways. No one is busy with appeasing either superiors or subordinates. A message is a message—whether good or bad. Such openness and honesty is absolutely necessary when running a risky business, such as an aircraft carrier, where small discrepancies can have fatal consequences. My experiences in the companies I have worked for is the same; besides, it impacts directly and positively on the bottom line.

Although businesses and other civil society organizations rarely have time to drill skills and procedures as military organizations do, the principle is an important consideration. Our processes were time consuming and costly because we were a large organization. Sending managers and employees to training courses and seminars for days on end is not inexpensive. But I always saw this as an investment—never an expense. Considering the results we achieved at both the SAS and Wilhelmsen companies, I'm convinced that it was worth every penny.

We had rare serious mishaps or accidents. But once it could have been disastrous. One of our larger ships was on the way into Sydney with a pilot on board. It was early morning and there was no indication that everything was not going to plan. The captain and his crew were in charge of all the ship's features, including speed. The pilot always knows the local waters and, in addition, knows how wind and currents can affect the ship.

We never really found out what went wrong. But something happened, for the ship entered the harbor at too great a speed and at the wrong angle. When the captain realized what was happening, he tried to reverse the ship with full engine power, but the huge colossus smashed into the pier. It hit a huge crane, which toppled over a warehouse. The devastation of the surrounding land had the appearance of a small disaster area.

Only the ship made it through practically unscathed. Fortunately, the collision occurred before the port workers had come to work in the morning: no person was injured. Had this happened during the day, it would have become a real disaster.

The captain was an experienced sailor on his first tour as captain. I was in Sydney when it occurred; when I met him on board, he was devastated. He was quite sure that he would be fired for gross misconduct: the captain is not free from responsibility as skipper even with a pilot on board. Everything that happens to the ship is the captain's responsibility, unless another ship causes a collision with his. But even then the captain must answer for his own ship's movements and what he did, if anything, to avoid the collision.

Hardly anyone would have opposed the unfortunate captain's removal of his obligations. But what would that have accomplished? This was a rare exception. Thus, we had no need to set an example, as might be necessary with sloppy cultures. The captain had been punished more than enough with all the maritime inquiries and other calamities with the local port authorities, not to mention his awareness of what the mistake had cost both the insurance company and the shipping company.

But just as important was that his anger and despair was so formidable that I thought, "If there is anything that man will never do again, it will be to enter into calm waters at too high a speed. And if there is something he will do, it will be to make sure that everyone on board follows all procedures to the letter at all times." In other words, we actually have an even better skipper, albeit at a high price. We could not afford to let him go. And that's what happened. The skipper continued his duties and sailed without any incidents the rest of his career.

I think this solution and the way we justified it resulted in a much more correct signal-effect in the organization than if we had let him go. There was nothing in the event that dictated anything other than that he had miscalculated. Afterward, the captain behaved in an exemplary fashion by taking 100 percent responsibility: first, by being available during all the investigations that were conducted, and second, by sharing his experience with other captains.

Shipping is not without risk; therefore, security procedures are at the same level as in aviation. Still, accidents do happen without anyone being held responsible. There may be chains of unfortunate circumstances, collective erroneous evaluations, and so on. Precisely in such organizations, it is important to show that those responsible don't necessarily lose their jobs, unless they have acted negligently. The consequence of implementing sanctions perceived as unreasonable often results in underreporting because people are afraid to admit when they have done something stupid or when they have seen others do so. Small deviations can form the basis for large mistakes later.

Nevertheless, this event was quite limited in scope in terms of what would be the real test of whether our company's value base held water. That came when one of our biggest Con-Ro ships, *Tampa*, became the center of an event which, apart from the Partnair accident, surpassed anything we had previously experienced in terms of drama, ethics and, not least, politics.

16
THE MOMENT OF TRUTH

Japan was an important market for Wilhelmsen for many years. Our presence went back over 100 years. Parallel with the buildup of the industrial development and the automotive industry offensive, this tiny island kingdom was also a leading shipbuilding nation, partly due to the prestigious Mitsubishi Heavy Industries group.

They gradually became known for their design capacity, which gave them the ability to deliver high-quality ships with enhanced state-of-the-art solutions. By the end of the 1970s, Mitsubishi had built two of the best Con-Ro ships in the Wilhelmsen fleet. Nevertheless, Wilhelmsen had not bound itself to any collaboration and had three other Con-Ro ships of the same type built at other yards in Japan.

In the first part of the 1990s, it was still profitable to combine Ro-Ro shipping with container freight on Con-Ro ships. But we needed to upgrade our fleet and increase capacity. Through our contact with Japan and Japanese shipyards, we renewed our contact with Mitsubishi. Even though we had not had active customer relations for almost a decade, the relationship was still good. Therefore, we initiated a partnership with Mitsubishi to develop and build what was the world's largest Con-Ro ship when it was named *Taronga* and launched in 1996.

The shipyard's design department had put immense effort into the construction of the ship and barely made money on the first delivery. The intention was to build more ships of the same type, and we had options on this. But before we got that far, we made the strategic decision to get out of the container market and focus 100 percent on Ro-Ro shipping. We asked if Mitsubishi would join in developing the new solely Ro-Ro ships, but they declined.

Although Mitsubishi was disappointed that we did not make use of the options, there was little we could do about it. As we developed and built the first ship, the market changed. Thus, the prerequisite for building ships of the same type no longer existed.

Instead, we developed and built four Ro-Ro ships of a new type at the Korean Daewoo shipyard. Our relationship with the Korean company functioned quite well, but we continued to maintain good contact with Mitsubishi through occasional meetings. As the market evolved further and load compositions changed, the need for new solutions increased. We saw a need to develop new Ro-Ro ships with more advanced features.

During our informal get-togethers with Mitsubishi, we openly discussed this new need; soon Mitsubishi was on board again. With the lesson from the first round of the Con-Ro ship still in recent memory, Mitsubishi made sure we weren't following a new fad. In return, we created a deeper basis for collaboration—something I think back on with the greatest satisfaction.

Thanks to what we learned about each other—both good and bad—a relationship of trust developed, which was so strong that we could even write sketches for solutions and specifications on napkins during late dinners and seal them with only a handshake. The official documents we read later were identical with what we had agreed to on the napkins.

I liked this way of doing business. It was in line with my intuitive management style and rarely came back to bite me. Fortunately, I had good people with me most of the time who could do the calculating, as I could when necessary. But in an open and equitable atmosphere that reigned during these business deals, where both suggestions and objections flowed seamlessly across the table, it was easier to trust my gut feeling. The main driving force was finding the best and most profitable solutions for both parties.

We developed a separate PIP together with our most important suppliers and business partners, such as those who provided port and terminal services. The program followed the same principle we had followed with our most important customers: we sat down with each at the management level and identified problem areas and improvement potential. When we agreed upon a common outlook, we created a plan of action based on specific measures. This plan also specified who should do what—and when. At the same time, we clarified roles and responsibilities in our common development process. In this way, we linked binding relationships to anyone with influence on the quality and efficiency of the services we provided. Immediate results were achieved in most places.

One of the challenges was anchoring these process-es at the appropriate organizational level. Sometimes we had to go right to the top. Other times, when responsi-bility was delegated to operational levels in the organi-zation, we found it better to deal with those involved at those levels. We had a dynamic relation with whomever we met. The most important thing was finding out where the decision-making authority was.

As CEO, I often found that many vendors had not done their research on our organization in advance and tried to sell ideas, products, and services at the wrong lev-el. Sometimes I agreed to meet people who were absolute-ly convinced they had something for which I had to make a decision. Then it would turn out that they should have approached someone several levels down the organiza-tion where the decision-making authority belonged.

When asked if, as CEO, I couldn't influence the deci-sion, I considered the meeting over. What would happen to the responsibility that we had worked so hard to anchor so far down in the organization if I intervened directly in individual cases? It would slowly short-circuit the organi-zation and ultimately sabotage responsibility.

We maintained the same open communication with our banks, Citibank, Deutsche Bank, DNB, and Kreditkassen (Nordea). They had been in on the rescue operation after the 1987 collapse in the offshore market. When conditions normalized and we began to make money during the 1990s, technically, we no longer needed to submit those results, budgets, investment plans, and analyses in order to conduct larger transactions.

Nevertheless, we continued doing it because we felt it added that extra peace of mind of having banks on our team. Through regular meetings where we met people in senior management at the appropriate decision-making level, we developed close relationships with the banks. We presented the status of our results, our plans, and expectations.

The most obvious benefit of this was that it was easy to obtain the services we needed when we contracted ships or invested in other projects. And we also received an abundance of good advice along the way. Banking and financial products evolve just like everything else. By keeping an open line, we could use the banks' skilled people as advisors. We never experienced abuse of confidentiality of information we provided, even though the banks also served a number of our competitors. Secrecy and non-disclosure historically make one considerably more susceptible to unwanted leaks.

For a number of years in Korea, we were represented by our partly owned subsidiary and partner, Barwil. The company had a very accomplished and loyal Korean owner and boss who had brilliantly taken care of our customers and our interests but whose business was not very extensive, even though the market increased considerably throughout the 1990s when the Korean industry, including the automotive industry, really came on the offensive.

When we took over the Norwegian America Line (NAL), we received a considerably greater footprint in the Korean market through Norwegian Specialized Auto Carriers (NOSAC), which was wholly owned by NAL. NOSAC had a separate office in Korea, had built up a close relationship with KIA, and transported its cars. Due to the merger with Wallenius, we got an even bigger representation in the country. Both NOSAC and Wallenius had built up good relations with the automotive industry and several manufacturers of construction machinery.

The other major Korean car manufacturer, Hyundai, had established its own shipping company, Hyundai Merchant Marine (HMM), focused primarily on the container market. It shipped the parent company's cars to some parts of the world but eventually needed more Ro-Ro capacity when car sales began to rise toward the end of the 1990s. KIA went bankrupt in 1998 and was taken over by the Hyundai group but continued as a separate brand.

We still transported KIA cars and had a good working relationship with the new owners. Meanwhile, HMM experienced that the container market was characterized by overcapacity and declining profitability. To save the company, they wanted to sell what they could: the car division. They contacted us and asked if we would take over that division. One reason was that we had developed a good relationship with HMM through one of Wilhelmsen's key executives, Jan Eivind Wang, from the time he was the leader of the NOSAC office in Seoul in the late 1980s. Personal relationships are very important; it is always advisable to take care of them.

Wallenius and Wilhelmsen bought 40 percent each for a total of 260 million USD and established a new company, Eukor (Europe-Korea), with the same share distribution. Hyundai went in with 20 percent.

The company was registered in Korea with a Swedish manager and a Norwegian financial director. The manager was the former head of the Wallenius office in Korea. Most of the remaining employees came from HMM and from Korea. However, Wallenius Wilhelmsen retained its office in Seoul since there was still a lot of business with customers in addition to Hyundai and KIA.

As with all our other acquisitions, we wanted to instill most of our management philosophy into the new company. But—and this was a big *but*—it had to be done much more gently, taking the Korean culture into account. Koreans are very capable and efficient but used to a more instructive and controlling management style. Thus, there would be no coaching in the traditional sense we practiced in the rest of the organization—the ideal method. Nevertheless, we finagled much of the responsibility factor, which was part of the essence of coaching, into Eukor, so people felt a stronger feeling of importance. At any rate, we noticed that well-being ran very high and that talented people at all levels wanted to work for the company. Eukor's large fleet ships cars from Hyundai and KIA throughout the whole world.

The mighty Chung family, who is the largest owner in the Hyundai group, was clearly pleased with the creation of Eukor. Not long after we established Eukor, they offered us 25 percent of the shares in Hyundai's logistics company, Glovis. That did not fit with the Wallenius family, but the Wilh. Wilhelmsen Group purchased the 25 percent for 100 million USD. When the company went public soon after that, it was valued at 50 percent over our purchase value. A few years later the value quadrupled.

However, the idea behind it had not been stock speculation. We had only two reasons for buying Glovis. One was to cement our relationship with the Hyundai group; the other was to get access to the logistics business. Viewed from our side, it was business. Viewed from the Koreans' side, it was perceived as a vote of confidence.

In 2009, the value of the shares in Glovis and Eukor was 850 million USD. In seven years, our 230 million USD expenditure had increased to 850 million. I could not help thinking about how a ship owner from little Norway on the other side of the globe could gain such a position in one of the world's leading industrial nations.

The most probable reason was the way we built and fostered our relationship with the Koreans. We had 100 percent respect for them and for what they were, and we tried to the best of our ability to follow their customs. We went with them on hard mountain tours up to the border of North Korea, ate their food, and attended concerts and theatrical performances they were proud to show off, but of which we understood nothing.

In like manner, we introduced them to the best of nature and culture we had in Norway when they visited us. This made for good chemistry. Even the biggest business deals are not primarily about millions of dollars but about meetings between people. We develop positive or negative energy at every meeting, which either helps strengthen or weaken one of the finest structures we humans can build together: confidence.

For over 100 years, Wilhelmsen had sailed regularly to Australia. It was, perhaps, the continent where we had built up one of the strongest organizations and where our fundamental values were just as strong as in Norway.

As the values of Wilhelmsen more clearly became the basis and guideline for business and customer-related dealings, the more robust the organization became—even when undesirable incidents arose. Critical situations test the essence of our values. A crisis is the very moment of truth where you are tested as to whether you are able to make the right decisions, even when under considerable pressure.

Such a situation arose with the ship, *Tampa*, which was en route from Australia to Singapore on August 25, 2001, carrying 1,100 containers on deck. Many of the containers were empty and Ro-Ro decks in the hull had little cargo. The ship, therefore, sailed easily on the sea. The weather was perfect. The sun was shining from an almost clear sky. It was one of those days on board when you felt nothing could happen.

The next day the ship would sail into the Sunda Strait of Indonesia, known for aggressive pirates. But crew members took precautions against them. They battened down the hatches, barricaded doors and ladders, and brought out flood lamps and water cannons to prevent possible nocturnal attackers from boarding. Behind the ship, 200 meters of thin wire was hung out, which would wrap around the propellers of attackers' boats if they tried to sneak up behind the ship and seek refuge under the stern.

Suddenly a Mayday message came in from the Australian rescue service. The message disclosed that the coast guard had observed another ship a few hours away which was probably in distress. The message confirmed it to be a small ship of 35 meters with over 80 people on board. HELP and SOS were written on the roof in uppercase letters. Of all the ships in the area, the *Tampa* was the closest to come to their aid.

Captain Arne Frode Rinnan didn't hesitate a second in ordering the new course when he received the message in his office under the bridge. On the high seas, there is one thing that comes before consideration of punctuality, service, customers, and shipping company: human life.

Rinnan was one of our most experienced captains. He ran away to sea as a deck boy in 1958; after that no job offer on land could keep him from becoming a sailor. At 60 years old, he was on his last regular tour with the *Tampa*. As it turned out, this trip would make him famous all over the world, not because fame was something he sought, but because a number of people in prominent positions showed that they did not have the same human values instilled in them as Rinnan and his outstanding crew did.

After four hours of sailing, the *Tampa* encountered a sorrowfully sinking ship; the small vessel drifted in pretty rough sea. It was taking on water after what had probably been an explosion in the engine room and wouldn't stay afloat much longer. There was only one solution: take everyone aboard the *Tampa*.

One by one, each passenger was lifted onto the gangway, which hung alongside the *Tampa*. It was difficult and dangerous work because the ships were out of sync on the sea. The operation was also considerably larger than expected: what was to have been 80 people on board turned out to be five times as many—a total of 438 people, of which 26 were women and 43 were children. These were people who had fled from Afghanistan, the Islamic Republic of Pakistan, and Sri Lanka. Conditions on board had been completely inhumane, with minimal food and water and hopeless toilet conditions. Few people could swim, and there were not enough life jackets.

Unexpectedly, the *Tampa*, which was certified for a crew of 27, suddenly had 465 people on board including the crew. Refugees were assembled on the container deck where tarpaulins were hung for shade. Amazingly, the onboard cook managed to provide food for everyone. Some were quite frail after horror-filled days on board the crowded, tiny craft. Several needed medical treatment.

The refugees soon chose five advocates who asked for a meeting with Rinnan. They thanked him for rescuing them and asked to be put ashore on Christmas Island, which was Australian territory and the nearest port. They made it clear that they could not go back to their home countries or to Indonesia or Singapore, where many of them had probably stayed illegally before human smugglers took them on board and embarked on the hazardous journey. For Rinnan and his crew, it was perfectly natural to go there rather than to continue the journey to Singapore or Indonesia, a solution we in management, of course, applauded.

That's when the real drama began and showed what people were truly made of. Australia had long been tired of virtually all ship refugees in the South China Sea landing on Australian soil, with many of them seeking and receiving asylum in the country. It was just prior to elections and Prime Minister John Howard, who was running for reelection, felt that it was high time to mark where he stood politically regarding the continuous flow of refugees into the country he led.

Thus, the same authorities who had asked the *Tampa* to come to the aid of the sinking ship, Rescue Coordination Center Australia, now refused the *Tampa* entry to Australian territorial waters. Despite the fact that Rinnan reported that several of the refugees, including two pregnant women, were in critical medical condition, he received no offers of medical attention.

But Rinnan could not be swayed. He sailed toward Christmas Island and demanded that RCC send a doctor. The doctor came when the *Tampa* finally anchored outside the Australian island. A group of heavily armed troops from the Special Air Service also boarded the ship and, contrary to international law and customs when human lives are at stake, tried to force it out of Australian waters.

Meanwhile, Wilhelmsen's Australian CEO, Peter Dexter, was under tremendous pressure from known and unknown people at high levels in the Australian government administration. Prime Minister Howard personally called Dexter twice to get his recalcitrant Norwegian captain to leave Australian waters. When that failed, he tried adopting an urgent law in the Australian Parliament to gain a clearer legal authority to send the *Tampa* back out into international waters. The bill suffered defeat.

Negotiations went on for several days. Meanwhile many of the refugees on board the *Tampa* suffered, even though the sickest got medical help and the crew did their best to take care of them. Eventually, some became threatening and aggressive. The heavily armed soldiers did not make the situation easier, although in one sense they represented security in the event the situation got out of control.

Captain Rinnan was unwavering in his demand that the refugees be allowed to go to Christmas Island. He received full support from those of us in management who handled the case through our emergency group at Lysaker, led by Operations Director Håvard Hareide. There was disagreement about what to do. The lives and health of those poor refugees came first. We gave little thought to how adversely it might affect our otherwise good relations, whether it was with customers who were waiting for their goods or with Australian authorities. Conversely, we appreciated the invaluable support from the Norwegian government, particularly through foreign minister Thorbjørn Jagland.

As the situation became public internationally, the pressure increased on the Australian government. There was no doubt about which side the international public opinion took. On August 31, six days after the refugees had been rescued from their small craft, even more troops boarded to force the *Tampa* out into international waters: Rinnan still refused. By now, he knew that a political solution of the case was impending.

On September 1, the parties came up with a solution that they all could live with. The refugees would be sent by an Australian troop carrier to Papua New Guinea. From there 150 of them would be transported to New Zealand and the rest to the tiny Republic of Nauru in the South Pacific, where there were a little over 10,000 people. On September 3, the refugees were transferred from the *Tampa* to a troop ship. The Australian police took care of the four smugglers who were responsible for having caused the hapless journey to begin with.

The episode resulted in several aftermaths. It turned out that the Australian military had bugged the ship throughout the whole drama, even conversations that took place between the *Tampa* and the Norwegian Embassy in Australia, and between the *Tampa* and the shipping company's emergency response group at Lysaker. The Australian Army also illegally monitored Wilhelmsen's and the insurance company's Australian lawyer when he discussed, among other things, taking civil action against the Australian State if the *Tampa* was forced out of Australian waters.

The Australian Defense Force apologized later to the lawyer about the illegal wiretap, but Prime Minister Howard could not see that he had done anything worthy of criticism: "We handled the *Tampa* according to international law, and I'm sorry that nothing was done to defend national interests," he said. The event revealed a lot of confusion between international and national provisions in matters like this.

Captain Rinnan was deservedly celebrated as a national and international hero during this affair. He received a number of accolades and awards for his steadfast and humane attitude toward the unfortunate people who had risked their lives trying to make a better life for themselves.

As a shipping line, I think we also won by sticking to our principles, even if some of our customers had to wait an extra week for their goods. A business always wins by putting concern for human dignity ahead of profit and politics. The way Captain Rinnan and the rest of the shipping line acted showed that our values were truly alive, even when under threat to act differently. "Lex the *Tampa*" has become a role model for most shipping companies.

17
ON THE FRONT LINE

On January 1, 2003, I took over as Group CEO from Wilhelm Wilhelmsen, who had led the company since Løddesøl had stepped down as group CEO to become chairman of the board. Now Wilhelm Wilhelmsen was chairman and Løddesøl was a board member.

I had no more desire for the CEO position at Wilh. Wilhelmsen than I had at SAS. The job as CEO of WWL had been more than exciting and educational with all the processes we had been through. But now the entire group was at a crossroads: important decisions had to be made requiring major change processes.

In practice, it meant no more than moving from the third to the fifth floor of the office building at Lysaker. As chairman of the board, Wilhelm Wilhelmsen was still my immediate supervisor. He and Løddesøl were very different, but both were very professional. We attended most meetings together but didn't see each other much when traveling; for safety reasons, we never flew on the same plane.

Wilh. Wilhelmsen was the sole shareholder in the two service companies, Barwil and Barber International— two of the largest global players in an industry that was still characterized by many small companies. On several occasions we had discussed merging the two companies, but each time it was pointed out that the companies were so different that it would be difficult for them to collaborate. This was one of the things I had been working on as deputy CEO at WW, where I was responsible for Wilhelmsen Lines and coordination of outside organizations. The merger with Wallenius shelved this work.

Barwil ran an agent business for a wide range of international shipping companies, which involved sales and marketing, managing ships in port, representing other shipping companies that did not have their own infrastructure, supplying goods to ships in port, along with integrated logistics services. Among other things, the company had accomplished great pioneer work in Black Sea countries where ship traffic had increased sharply after the fall of the Iron Curtain in 1989, but where varied standards existed for all types of maritime services that ships needed in port.

Barber International dealt mainly as a ship manager; that is, they operated ships on behalf of other shipping companies with responsibility for technical maintenance, operation, and crewing.

After a new review of the companies in the spring of 2004, we saw that the market had changed enough that there would probably be large benefits to merging the companies. This would provide a stronger platform for all of WW's global activities in terms of growth and development. Thus, the board supported initiating a process that would go one step further. The project was named "One Voice" and determined all aspects of a possible merger.

Again, we went to customers for their opinion of the two service companies' delivery capabilities. The result was similar to what we had found out in Wallenius Wilhelmsen: the quality of services varied. With two independent organizations in which interaction between departments varied, we again failed to reach a high-enough level in the customers' decision-making bodies. Customers purchased individual services and goods instead of coming to us for a total solution for deliveries so we could help develop customer purchases at a strategic level.

With increasingly specialized ships, there were greater demands for customizing all kinds of services. We saw that it would probably be easier to meet these demands if we gathered all services under the same umbrella. Based on these perspectives, the net gains of a merger came to around 10 million USD.

In September 2004, we decided to merge the companies under the name of Wilhelmsen Maritime Services (WMS) as of January 1, 2005. The CEO of the new company was Dag Schjerven, whose professional background included industry experience from Dyno Industries. He would lead the process of gathering all service companies into a single maritime trading house with 3,100 employees in 250 offices located in 65 countries.

WMS could supply everything from shipping agencies, bunker fuel, and insurance, to IT solutions for logistics services, ship operations, crewing, and advanced consulting for ship construction and maintenance. We targeted the company's vision considerably higher than

in the past. We were to be the "Shaper of the Maritime
Service Industry."

I'm not sure where the formulation of this vision
came from. Like most other good ideas, it was probably
the result of teamwork. What we liked the most about it
was that it was dynamic and clearly pointed to the future of development. At the time, no other maritime services providers had defined such a comprehensive and
future-oriented proposal for customers. Simultaneously,
it forced us to be continually on the offensive.

With this worldwide company, the Wilhelmsen
Group was about to get a solid platform to stand on, in
addition to shipping routes. This was in line with strategic guidance in reducing our vulnerability. But now, tank,
bulk, container, and offshore ships were replaced with
services directly linked to the core business and which
proceeded along the same route we had taken during the
development of logistics products.

As a result, it was natural to review the entire Wilhelmsen Group's values and visions. We found our values to be very well adapted. We had already achieved our
old vision, which declared that we should be foremost in
taking the lead. Wilh. Wilhelmsen had become the world
leader in its field. Now we needed to find what our future
goals would be. We found the answer in our new subsidiary, WMS. We only had to remove one word: *service*. Thus,
the new vision became "Shaper of the Maritime Industry."

We still lacked muscle in this new maritime mecha-
nism. One participant that could complete the body was

Unitor Ships Service, which Wilhelmsen had tried to purchase in 1986 but which the crisis in the shipping company had prevented. After that there had been some discussions about coordinating the Barwil and Unitor services, but nothing ever came of it.

Some on the Wilhelmsen board were hesitant to purchase another company, which also conducted industrial production of chemicals, even though they were intended for the maritime ship market. They believed it was still too far afield from Wilhelmsen's core business—shipping. Nevertheless, they agreed to acquire the company.

After a hectic six months, WMS grew to 4,500 employees with 340 offices in 80 countries. In addition, we had 7,500 sailors in the global crew pool. In reality, at this point there were three companies to be merged because the integration process between Barber International and Barwil was not yet finalized. That was actually good, for it made liberal thinking possible when it came to how we would build up the new organization.

We followed the principle we had followed for all the previous mergers and acquisitions of which I had been a part. We created a totally new organization chart, removing all managers from their functions, and defined 35 new management positions that would be filled with the most competent people—regardless of which company they came from.

This resulted in more former Unitor managers than WMS managers receiving central leadership roles. This led to some discontent among former Barwil managers.

Since they had belonged to the purchasing party, they assumed that they would sit in the driver's seat in the new organization. Now they wondered who had actually purchased whom. Some quit. Others who could not come to terms with our pragmatic and competence-based selection of leaders were asked to find another job.

Despite the comprehensive information process along the way, it was possible that we had not been astute enough to ingrain the merger process in all previous key people in Barwil, where resistance to the merger was the greatest. Thus, we hadn't reconciled people's expectations to the new company. Perhaps the acquisition and merger with Unitor was a factor for a lot of people who had struggled with accepting the Barber and Barwil merger.

Initially, Unitor did not have the same formal attitude to values and value-based management. Our cultures were quite different. The subsequent integration process was carefully planned; it took a year and a half. We set up 740 objectives to attain along the way. One of the overall objectives was reducing the calculated costs of 40 million USD. Therefore, 400 employees were offered early retirement, termination packages, or jobs in other parts of the WW Group. Meanwhile, we worked on the revenue side, which led to the eventual hire of 500 new employees in other positions in order to acquire the appropriate competencies.

We had all of the advantages of our past value processes. We undertook a review of the basic Wilhelmsen values and found that they matched our vision, the market situation, and the delivery expertise that WMS needed. During preparation and implementation of our objectives, we examined ongoing issues related to our vision and values:

- Does it aid in putting us foremost in development of the maritime industry?
- Is this in the best interest of our customers?
- Does this help create increased commitment and recognition?
- Is it innovative?
- Are we learning from what we do? How do we apply the learning?
- Is this optimal management of company resources?
- How do we cooperate across former company boundaries and methods of working?

Another important instrument along the way was the WW Academy, which we created in 1999, where we used speakers, content, and tools from the Center for Creative Leadership. The precursor to the academy was a series of evening classes offered to all employees so they could get to know the company and the industry better. Even though the courses were held in the evening and no one was paid to attend, they were almost always fully booked. The most likely reason was that we had created a company culture where people viewed learning and acquiring the greatest insight and knowledge a professional necessity and a factor for job satisfaction.

We called the WW Academy the company's strategic educational center. All managers and employees from around the world went through programs tailored to their roles and responsibilities in the organization with the purpose of clarifying those positions and understanding them in the light of Wilhelmsen's vision and values, customer perspectives, and ways of working.

We put 300-400 managers and employees through the academy per year. One important effect from this was that people from around the world became acquainted and learned each other's cultures. In practice, the WW Academy was an exercise in multicultural understanding and development of an international team spirit, which would otherwise have been difficult to create.

Through a mix of in-house and contractual strengths, everyone received a tailored educational offer that we fully controlled. This produced a more superior effect in contributing to the company's development than sending employees to various management courses or other external training courses, which could teach a person methods and techniques but lacked the company's mission statement and cultural standpoint.

We came out with online learning programs early—not primarily to save money but because it represented an innovation in line with Wilhelmsen's values and made it possible to reach further into the entire organization. This was very successful and has continuously been developed to what it is today: a complete training program for managers and employees.

Together with Barber International we also developed a separate innovation program where we sent selected managers and employees to Silicon Valley, Singapore, and other places to learn from the most innovative communities there. They returned with a number of good ideas; unfortunately, most fell on deaf ears.

We in the leadership group had to take ownership of that. We had simply forgotten to prepare the rest of the organization for a possible influx of revolutionary products and customer developments, along with the need to discuss them. Thus, several came back feeling that what they said was not heard, and they felt no support for their newly acquired knowledge. I doubt that it would have been difficult to reconcile expectations for this in advance. But without adequate help from managers in the system, it was difficult to implement the projects. The consequence was that many talented participants in the innovation program quit Wilhelmsen.

It is easy to believe that when you know or have acknowledged something, others know it too. But if you fail to pull people with you from the start, ideas might be great but will never gain ground. We probably did better with the actual integration process, for we expected that to be difficult. We thought getting approval for new ideas from the innovation mecca, Silicon Valley, would be easy. It was not. Perhaps that is one of the reasons we did not progress far enough in the WMS and Unitor integration processes.

As long as the integration process continued, we conducted regular information meetings for all managers and employees. I attended all of these meetings, using every opportunity to restate our vision and our values. I continually tried to find new ways to make them relevant to keep from boring myself and those to whom I spoke. The tighter I linked our vision and values to our customers and our business basis, the easier it got—just as I did with the new vision at Wilhelmsen Maritime Services and the last round we had on Wilhelmsen values where we had set the five basic values.

It was important to justify that these were a consequence of the company's vision, business ideas, and values, especially when there was a need to inform others about changes that had implications for their roles and responsibilities in the organization, and which changes concerned people. That the value base worked in such situations, I felt was proof that it had been an integral part of the organization and not just decoration.

18
FULL CIRCLE

Now, when I have the opportunity to reflect from a distance on why things went better at Wilhelmsen than at SAS, I see different patterns for which I can take neither responsibility nor credit, but which depended considerably more on how the organization or the market developed. Yet, I see several similarities in how we ran the processes.

When Carlzon lost his footing at SAS, the organization became more like the culture I encountered when I started at Wilhelmsen. The distance between management and coworkers increased and, with it, the distance to customers. Carlzon's most ambitious strategies were not anchored in customers or coworkers but in his personal level of ambition, which eventually flew too high. SAS would no longer be the best for customers and the best company to work in, but the greatest. Why? Because that's what the CEO wanted, and he'd gotten the board and the largest part of the management team to join him on the journey.

In Wilh. Wilhelmsen, we never worked to be the biggest; we strove to be the best. It was never the intent to have the most tonnage or the greatest number of field offices. Our last vision, "Shaper of the Maritime Industry," was qualitative and customer focused, although, of course, it presupposed certain quantitative capacities. Size was a means, not an end.

When the SAS owners realized that the new goals of the 1990s were too high, and that they were unlikely to achieve them, much of the organization once again fell back to the age-old wrinkles that had survived the turn-around operations of the 1980s. The trade unions were the same. Middle managers, who had not yet signed on to the new processes, quickly found themselves at home in their old positions. The new board and new top management went back to the situation before Carlzon's fairy-tale results in the 1980s. Organizationally, the company had regressed 10 years but with a fleet and a crew that were adapted to a completely different level.

It could travel in one direction only: downward. And with the downturn came desperation, which has more or less characterized SAS since: cost cutting and more cost cutting—all in the wrong areas. One infusion of capital followed another. But worst of all, products and concepts, which were intended to compete in every direction, left customers in greater doubt about the kind of company they were flying with.

In both Wilhelmsen Lines and later in the entire Wilh. Wilhelmsen Group, all the processes developed in the same direction and were very clear for everyone: how can we build an organization and a culture that consistently progresses higher up in the customer's value chain? That is what we actually did at SAS Cargo with the aquaculture industry and with EuroClass and first business class for full-paying business customers. I'm sure there would still have been great development potential in these areas if the company had put the customers—and not their own ambitions—in the best seats.

The processes at the Wilhelmsen Group most likely went deeper and were considerably more binding in all aspects of the organization. At all times, the processes began with top management, who then worked outwardly to the customer front, with their own coworkers and affiliates, subcontractors, and other business partners. I conducted the introduction to all gatherings and seminars to give them authority, regardless of what level they were.

These processes quickly showed who the team players were and who resisted or resigned. Instead of allowing them to stand on the sidelines or work behind the scenes for other solutions—as happened at SAS in the first turnaround during the early 1980s and to where it slipped back at the end of Carlzon's tenure—they had a choice to commit themselves or find something else to do. The result was that some quit, including people in key positions. Such must be expected.

During mergers and large acquisitions in Wilhelmsen, we always reset the organization and started everyone on equal terms in the new company. And we did the restructuring processes as quickly as possible. It rarely took longer than a month for the new organization to start up. This way, uncertainty and un-culture could not steal energy, ingenuity, and vigor while the pieces fell into place. Meanwhile, we conducted frequent information meetings for all employees so that they always had answers to the most important questions that managers and employees ultimately ask when they go through organizational changes, including: *What's in it for me?*

When SAS took over Braathens, the employees from the two former companies received different terms and conditions, and not enough work was done to unite the two cultures. That reinforced the conflict. It wasn't fun if you had to stand on a stack of pallets in a hangar and try to inspire the employees. Many of the managers rarely showed their faces in the organization, if ever. So a lot of air went out of the balloon that had powered SAS to be the world's best airline.

In the 1980s, SAS was Norway's most attractive place to work. Pride characterized the Braathens culture. By the beginning of the 2000s, several studies showed that employees had a worse view of the new SAS Braathens company than outsiders. The latter feared losing competition and increased prices because SAS and Braathens held a virtual monopoly. Passengers, however, were still satisfied with flying with SAS.

In Wilhelmsen, we saw the opposite tendency. Climate studies showed that employee satisfaction increased proportionally with clarity of the value processes. Best of all: when we looked at the correlation between the results of climate surveys and financial performance, they were completely compatible. The greater the satisfaction, the greater the goal achievement. This, of course, was because the climate processes were rooted solidly in the development of our customers and their needs.

It amazes me that leaders don't show more interest in examining such simple correlations, rather than hiring expensive consultant companies that change the organization chart based on short-term attention to the business's efficiency and profitability.

After being involved in all the change processes at SAS and Wilhelmsen, it has become evident to me that the driving force in an organization must be achieving profitability by creating the greatest possible value to customers. The combination of good results and satisfied customers creates so much positive energy that it becomes a joy to go to work, something I am convinced has been an equally important driver for me.

The day a leader dreads going to work is the day that leader should stay home to avoid spreading frustration through the organization. Leader attitude is contagious. Perhaps so much so that I daresay, without shame: A leader has exactly the employees he or she deserves.

www.ingramcontent.com/pod-product-compliance
Lightning Source LLC
Chambersburg PA
CBHW031406180326
41458CB00043B/6640/J